LETTERS TO THE CHURCHES

1 and 2 TIMOTHY, TITUS

BIBLE GUIDES

The twenty-two volumes

★ already published

BIBLE GUIDES

General Editors: William Barclay and F. F. Bruce

No. 18

LETTERS TO THE CHURCHES

1 and 2 TIMOTHY, TITUS

by

MORTON S. ENSLIN

*Professor of Biblical Languages
and Literature,
St. Lawrence University,
Canton, New York*

Published jointly by

LUTTERWORTH PRESS
LONDON

ABINGDON PRESS
NEW YORK AND NASHVILLE

First published 1963

Printed in Great Britain by
Cox & Wyman Ltd., London, Fakenham and Reading

GENERAL INTRODUCTION

THE AIM of Bible Guides is to present in 22 volumes a total view of the Bible, and to present the purpose, plan and power of the Scriptures.

Bible Guides are free from the technicalities of Biblical scholarship but are soundly based on all the generally accepted conclusions of modern Bible research.

They are written in clear, simple, straightforward English. Each author has worked to a comprehensive editorial pattern so that the 22 volumes form a concise conspectus of the Bible.

THE AIM

The aim of Bible Guides is to offer a "guide" to the main themes of each book (or group of books) rather than a commentary on the text of the book. Through Bible Guides the Bible itself will speak its message, reveal its power and declare its purpose.

Bible Guides is essentially an undertaking for non-theologically equipped readers who want to know what the Bible is about, how its various parts came to be written and what their meaning is to-day. But the preacher, teacher, educator and expositor of all ranges of the Christian Church will find Bible Guides a series of books to buy and study. They combine the modern knowledge of the Bible together with all the evangelical zeal of sound Biblical expression—and all done in a handy readable compass.

EDITORIAL PLAN

In our suggestions to the writers of the various books we were careful to make the distinction between a "commentary" and a "guide". Our experience is that an adequate commentary on a book of the Bible requires adequate space and on the part of the student some equipment in the scholarly lore and technicalities of Biblical research. A "guide", however, can be both selective and compressed and do what it sets out to do—guide the reader in an understanding of the book. That has been, and is, our aim.

As general editors we have had a good deal of experience among the various schools of Biblical interpretation. We are constantly surprised at the amount of common Biblical understanding which is acceptable to all types of Christian tradition and churchmanship. We hope that our Bible Guides reflect this and that they will be widely used, and welcomed as a contribution to Biblical knowledge and interpretation in the twentieth century.

THE WRITERS

The writers of Bible Guides represent a widely selected area of Biblical scholars, and all of them have co-operated enthusiastically in the editorial plan. They conceive their work to be that of examination, explanation and exposition of the book(s) of the Bible each is writing about. While they have worked loyally to the pattern we suggested they have been completely free in their presentation. Above all, they have remembered the present power and appeal of the Bible, and have tried to present its message and its authority for life to-day. In this sense Bible Guides is, we think, a fresh venture in the popular understanding of the Scriptures, combined as it is with the scholarly skill of our company of writers. We owe our thanks also to our publishers and their editors, Dr. Emory Stevens Bucke of the Abingdon Press of New York and Nashville, and Dr. Cecil Northcott of the Lutterworth Press of London. Their careful management and attention to publishing detail have given these Bible Guides a world wide constituency.

WILLIAM BARCLAY
F. F. BRUCE

CONTENTS

AUTHOR'S FOREWORD

THIS IS in no sense another commentary on the Epistles to Timothy and Titus—the "Pastoral Epistles". There are many such, each with its own values. Instead, in line with the intent of the series of which this is a part, the attempt has been made to indicate the main themes and contributions of these three little books, not for the purpose of making it unnecessary to read them, but rather for the precisely opposite purpose, to arouse a keener desire to read them with a fresh interest and concern.

It is a pity that for many people there is the feeling that it is their "duty to read the Bible". Too often that makes the reading drudgery and lessens the likelihood of discoveries which might well prove of abiding value. Many is the book which has forever lost its value for the student because it was prescribed reading. They approached it under a sense of compulsion, with an I-dare-you-to-interest-me attitude, and the dare was, of course, not realized. Too often this has been true of the Bible. To many the idea never seems to occur that it is an interesting book—better said, library of books—that it was produced by men and women, very like ourselves, facing their problems, and reaching their solutions; that it is a record both of their triumphs and failures, their insights and their blind spots; and that the resultant saga, when approached aright, can be found to be no longer a religious chore, but a real and fascinating adventure.

The attempt is made in the following pages to encourage such a reading by presenting these little epistles not only as a small part of the Bible but as giving an unforgettable picture of men and women, not unlike ourselves, at one of the many crossroads of history, confronted by a new set of ideas and values in seeming sharpest clash with their inheritance from the past. In order to see what these little books are it is necessary to see what they are not. Only so can they take their proper place as an important if modest chapter in a story both old and new. No attempt is made in these pages to propound new theories or to solve old problems. Rather the attempt is made to indicate the reason that every time I re-read these pages from the past I find them increasingly fragrant and definitely worth the reading, and that I cannot escape the feeling that though their author was writing for his own day and generation, back in the second century, many of his words, so tinctured with a common-sense sobriety which never waxes old, may be pondered with profit by us to-day.

MORTON S. ENSLIN

PART I

THE LETTERS AND THEIR BACKGROUND

THE LETTERS AND THEIR BACKGROUND

CHRISTIANITY began, and has always continued, a missionary religion. Its mainspring has been the imperative demand, "The world for Christ in this generation; so much to do, so little time."

It started as a movement within Judaism—among Jews and for Jews. The overpowering confidence of Jesus that the end was at hand, God's long-deferred promise to Israel was speedily to be fulfilled, the long-dreamed-for Kingdom of heaven was immediately to dawn, had become the confidence of many who had heard His words and were convinced that He was a prophet sent by God—*the* prophet long ago prophesied and promised by Moses.

God's Promise in Jesus

His tragic death on the bleak hill outside Jerusalem's walls had not destroyed this confidence. Instead it had intensified it. God had promised. Jesus was His chosen messenger. His enemies had not triumphed. The prophet had not been vanquished. God, not the high priest or the Roman hireling governor, was the ruler. The death of His spokesman had been but another example of blind and wicked, but fruitless, opposition to the Most High. Jesus had not been cursed by God, as His enemies were claiming the scripture made certain (Deuteronomy 21: 23); instead God's blessing had been, and still was, upon Him and His work. He had triumphed over death, was even now with God in heaven speedily to return in triumph.

The Son of man of whom Jesus had so constantly spoken, of

whose momentary appearance as final judge He had been so sure—this Son of man was Jesus Himself. They had thought He had been speaking of another; now in the light of the crucifixion and of its aftermath of renewed confidence they were convinced that Jesus had been constantly referring to Himself. Thus in the days following Calvary was born the confidence which was to remain through the centuries a central part of Christian belief: the return of Jesus, His second coming—no longer "in lowly pomp . . . to die", but in majesty to judge and rule. In the time between—a very short interval while they would all be alive—they must strive that when the Son of man returned He would find faith in the earth.

From the very first the movement was a success. As crowds had hung on Jesus' words, electrified by His burning and undaunted confidence; so in the following months and years His followers found instant response to their impassioned repetitions of His clarion call to repent and make themselves ready for God's new Kingdom soon to dawn. To those in positions of wealth and power their word continued a menace and outrage, even as had the same word when sounded by the Prophet Himself. To many in Palestine, uncushioned by wealth or education and to whom life's daily round was very hard, this vision of the new age, easily seen as the fulfillment of God's promise to Abraham, was highly attractive. Soon God would be seen by all as the ruler of His people, not Rome and quisling high priests.

As the months and years wore on, certain changes were inevitable. In essence the central message remained the same: the speedy dawning of the Kingdom and the return of the one destined to be the king. Many echoes of that burning confidence remain. The constant petition in the prayer, "Thy kingdom come"; the passionate plea, "Amen, come, Lord Jesus!" the persistent tradition, surely born in that first generation, that Jesus had promised, "Truly . . . there are some standing here who will not taste death before they see the kingdom of God come with power"—all these, and they are but a few of many, indicate the nature of the first Christian confidence.

But there were many Jews who failed to respond. The leaders had viewed the passionate claim of the Prophet as a menace to law and order, which might easily lead to wide rebellion and the loss of the many privileges granted by Rome. In consequence they had contrived His death, not because they did not understand His word but because they did and trembled at the storm which at any moment might break loose.

Their opposition to the continued efforts of the crucified prophet's followers, who found ready response to this preaching (as such stories as that of the crowds at the first Pentecost make clear), is surely natural. In addition, the sense of outrage felt by the religious leaders towards one who had dared to consider himself the mouthpiece of God, when they *knew* that for centuries God had spoken to His people through the Scriptures He had given them, continued towards the prophet's followers. Did not the Scriptures make crystal-clear that all who were hanged on a tree were accursed of God? Did this not make certain that Jesus had been under God's curse? that otherwise God would not have permitted those who fancied themselves the rulers to be successful? Thus the success of the followers of the crucified prophet in gaining new recruits did not prove God's favor. Instead it was but another instance of the wicked flourishing (momentarily) as the green bay tree.

In addition, the preaching of these early followers was most offensive; in a word, highly insulting. Not yet had the idea arisen that the death of Jesus was but a part of God's plan, that, as later confidence expressed itself in a word attributed to Jesus, His death was a ransom for many. Instead, in those early years before men like Paul joined the movement, the death of Jesus was regarded—and placarded—as a horrid crime. This early emphasis

17

is very clear. The word in the mouth of the martyred Stephen is its epitome:

"You stiff-necked people, uncircumcised in heart and ears, you always resist the Holy Spirit. As your fathers did, so do you. Which of the prophets did not your fathers persecute? And they killed those who announced beforehand the coming of the Righteous One, whom you have now betrayed and murdered, you who received the law as delivered by angels and did not keep it" (Acts 7: 51-53).

The Crucified's Followers

Small wonder that we have early stories of men like Philip and Peter finding a remove to Samaria and to cities like Joppa and Caesarea, on the Mediterranean coast, advisable. The account of the early days of the Christian mission given in the first half of the Book of Acts is of necessity very brief and incomplete; it nonetheless makes very clear that the start of the Gentile mission was both gradual and unplanned, was in no small part due to the same suspicion and hostility which had sent Jesus to the cross.

Nor is it to be wondered at that, as the years went by, those followers who remained in Jerusalem became increasingly conservative and insistent upon the observance of ancestral Jewish rites and practices. James, the brother of Jesus, apparently of a distinctly conservative type, replaces Peter as the head of the Jerusalem group. Those who remained in Jerusalem were devoted to their crucified leader and sought to continue His work, but they became increasingly suspicious of their brethren who were reported to be careless or even willful in their disregard of circumcision and other demands of the Law of Moses.

During these years of mission preaching and expanding horizons a new figure made his appearance on what may be styled a little beforehand "the Christian scene": Saul of Tarsus: persecutor, champion, and martyr. Of his early life almost nothing is known. "Circumcised on the eighth day, of the people of Israel, of the tribe of Benjamin, a Hebrew born of Hebrews; as to the law a Pharisee, as to zeal a persecutor of the church, as to righteousness under the law blameless"—that is his own pen portrait (Philippians 3 : 5f.).

While in Damascus, where he was striving to do God service, he suffered a right-about-face, henceforth to be the devoted champion of the One he had sought to destroy. Of the nature of this conversion much has been written, but little known. The story of Acts, thrice repeated with varying details, would seem a secondary amplification of his own terse word: "But when he who had set me apart before I was born, and had called me through his grace, was pleased to reveal his Son to me, in order that I might preach him among the Gentiles, I did not confer with flesh and blood, nor did I go up to Jerusalem to those who were apostles before me, but I went away into Arabia; and again I returned to Damascus" (Galatians 1 : 15–17).

The basic fact of the conversion would seem to be: Saul became convinced that those whom he was combating were right. Jesus had not been cursed by God, as Calvary had seemed to him to prove. Instead, He had been raised from the dead, was now at God's right hand, soon to return to consummate the change He had heralded. That the right-about-face was the result of dissatisfaction with the Law of Moses, as has often been assumed, is most unlikely. Rather it would seem that he had been forced, quite against his will, to an approval of the quality of life shown by those whom he was seeking to destroy. They were, he was forced to admit, doing God's service and were under His blessing. Hence, since God never changes, His blessing had been with the movement since its start. In a word, God had blessed Jesus, despite the fact that He had been crucified.

That this revolutionary change was accompanied by some deeply moving experience is most probable. Many scholars have seen in the narrative in 2 Corinthians 12: 1–10—surely Paul was this "man in Christ"—a reference to his conversion. At any rate, he became convinced, as many a prophet before him, that God had chosen him as His mouthpiece and had furnished him with His message. Of course his fellow Jews, blinded as he himself had hitherto been, would see the light once he had announced to them what was now so clear to him.

They did not. Instead, the cross remained to most of his Jewish hearers a stumbling block. Convinced as he now was of the divine truth of his God-given message, he was confronted by the question: Why? Why did his fellow Jews fail to see what to him was so crystal-clear? And the answer was easy, if tragic. It was the Law: "Cursed be every one who hangs on a tree." It was this which was holding them, as it had him, from walking in the divine light. Here was the real point of conflict. Here then must be his constant emphasis.

In the Paul we know—the earliest of his letters is at least fifteen years after this shattering experience at Damascus—the results of this first decision are clear. "Jesus Christ and him crucified" had become his central theme. The Law of Moses and the Christian gospel were set in tragic contrast. This clash had arisen, not as is often supposed because Paul had earlier been a lukewarm Jew, already chafing under the Law's demands. Instead, it was the result of Jewish opposition—their continued inability to hurdle the stumbling block which for him now no longer existed.

In his letters we find him primarily an "apostle to the Gentiles". As he looked back over the years, he was certain that it was God's leading, not his own choice, which had set him on that path. That this "leading" had been the result of constant Jewish deafness and growing hostility, not the instant decision in Damascus years before, is certainly highly likely.

The Paul we know from his letters and the later chronicle in Acts was a tireless traveler, constantly proclaiming his gospel through Asia Minor and the cities to the west of the Aegean. As a result of his work Christian groups—churches—were established in many strategic urban centres: Philippi, Thessalonica, Berea, Corinth, Ephesus, to mention but a few. Nor was he a mere traveling evangelist, here to-day, gone to-morrow. We have erred in overstressing his role as a theologian to the extent that we have failed to see his most lasting contribution. Paul had the amazing knack of welding converts together into what were to prove lasting groups. In many of the cities he visited, notably Corinth and Ephesus, he remained for extended periods. In these centres, working at his trade to meet his needs—no huckster of the gospel, he: "For you remember our labor and toil, brethren; we worked night and day, that we might not burden any of you, while we preached to you the gospel of God" (1 Thessalonians 2 : 9)—he not only welded together and gave a firm foundation to the local converts but reached out into the surrounding areas—as far as Illyricum from Corinth, to such towns as Colossae and Laodicea in the Lycus valley from Ephesus—through journeys both of his own and of his trusted comrades and lieutenants.

And when Paul moved on from one centre to another, he did not lose contact with his converts. Not infrequently he returned for another stay; but—and this is of the utmost importance—in addition he wrote letters to these churches of which he was "bereft, for a short season, in person not in heart". This habit of the devoted master builder of churches, of keeping in contact with his converts by occasional letters, gave us our first Christian scriptures; for Paul's letters surely antedate by many years all the other writings in the New Testament.

That Paul thought of his letters to the churches of Corinth, Thessalonica, Philippi, Galatia, or Rome as being Scripture, parts of the Bible, is utterly improbable. Christians had a Bible, and it was to them all-complete. It was what we style the Old Testament, universally regarded as completely different from any other book: the complete and final word of God, not men. Paul came, as has been already suggested, to an estimate of the Law which scandalized many conservative Jewish Christians, but this did not in the slightest affect his reverence and regard for the Scriptures. He was convinced, as was every Jew and early Christian, that in the Scriptures was to be found God's all-complete revelation to mankind. And in this revelation was the clear prediction, for all who had eyes to see, of the Christian mission and its crucified and risen Lord. To think of adding to this book—God's greatest gift to men—would have seemed so blasphemously absurd as to be quite unthinkable.

The End was at Hand

Nor were his letters for the purpose of providing later generations with useful knowledge. There would be no future generations. The end was at hand, might dawn at any moment. No one can read his letters without finding that confidence the mainspring of Paul's concern. "We shall not all sleep, but we shall all be changed, in a moment, in the twinkling of an eye, at the last trumpet. For the trumpet will sound, and the dead will be raised imperishable, and we shall be changed" (1 Corinthians 15: 51f.). It was this conviction, which he shared with all early Christians as the direct bequest from their crucified Lord, that drove Paul for twenty years "on frequent journeys, in danger from rivers, danger from robbers, danger from my own people, danger from Gentiles, danger in the city, danger in the wilderness, danger at sea, danger from false brethren; in toil and hardship, through many a sleepless night" (2 Corinthians 11 : 26f.). So much to do, so little time !

This view of the future—the sand of the cosmic hour-glass almost run out—which was as passionately held by our early brethren as it seems impossibly grotesque to many to-day, did not in the slightest affect the solidity of the structure Paul produced. He might, and certainly did, believe the world was going to end on the morrow. He worked and taught as though it would last forever ! Whenever converts, with a less solid foundation, sought to lie back on their oars and have support in the waiting-time from their neighbors who "could not take it with them", Paul's word was immediate and clear : they were to live quietly, mind their own affairs, work with their hands to command the respect of outsiders and be dependent on nobody (1 Thessalonians 4 : 11f.).

Nonetheless, although none were in laziness to capitalize upon it, the end was at hand, to come "like a thief in the night". Thus, to revert to an earlier word, Paul's letters were not written for a future generation. There would be none. Instead they were specific, and often detailed, answers to particular problems which he had learned were troubling his churches. At times the group concerned had written him, indicating difficulties which had arisen and asking his advice. At other times word had come indirectly. 1 Corinthians would seem his answer to information received in both these ways (7 : 1 ; 1 : 11). His replies were careful appraisals of the situations reported and the words which he would have spoken orally could he have returned in person.

Specific Letters to Specific People

Thus in the truest sense of the word Paul's letters were precisely that; letters, not epistles. This distinction is an important one, for in later years Christians were to produce "epistles", in form letters, but intended for a far wider audience, with the personal relationship—an "I" to a "you"—entirely absent. Both types of writing were well known in the ancient world: the personal and intimate letters of Cicero on the one hand: the rhetorical and careful *Moral Letters* of Seneca on the other.

All of the genuine letters of Paul, with the possible exception of "Romans", are of this former type. They are not intended for all Christians everywhere, nor do they seek to give a balanced survey of Paul's central beliefs. Instead they are specific replies to specific problems: why he had not returned, as he had promised, to Thessalonica; Philemon's responsibility as a Christian to his erring but now repentant slave Onesimus.

Paul was not writing to strangers. Instead he was writing to folk with whom he had been in intimate, often lengthy, fellowship. They knew his mind on many points. Where no uncertainty existed, there was no need of instruction. Instead he concerned himself with problems which had arisen among these immature Christians and by which they were perplexed or misled.

Failure to recognize this all-important distinction has often led to unnecessary confusion. On many central points Paul has little or nothing to say, for here there is no perplexity; he had treated this in detail in his oral preaching. Some matters upon which we to-day would welcome more light still remain in the shadows, for apparently his readers knew those answers as we do not. On the other hand, his careful and detailed words, which he was forced to write when he gladly would have hastened back, had that been possible, provide us again and again with intimate and firsthand information about many of the problems perplexing our early brethren and leading their elder brother in Christ to attempt—from a distance of miles but not of concern—to set them straight. Many of the problems which once concerned them, master and converts alike, have solved themselves

24

in the course of the years and seem singularly dated to us to-day. Others, which now convulse us, had not arisen to perplex the stumbling Corinthians and foolish Galatians. But when read with understanding, these so personal letters from the distant past not only reveal—often in very intimate detail, as evidenced by the lengthy correspondence with Corinth—vivid pictures of what may be styled "Christian life in primitive churches", but also provide us with down-to-earth insights, still of value to-day, untarnished by the lapse of centuries, into problems which persistently remain.

In an earlier paragraph mention was made of "Romans" as being in part unlike the other Pauline letters. It is. Paul had never been in Rome and felt no personal responsibility for the Christians there. He did not "build upon another's man's foundation" (Romans 15: 20). In his hope of visiting the far west to continue his work in untilled fields as far as Spain, he planned to make a brief visit in Rome—not as a teacher but as a traveler breaking his journey among Christian friends. His letter to them was thus not dictated by the desire to set them straight on matters to them confused. Instead it was to indicate to them the sort of man he was and the reason for his coming. Thus "Romans" is, as all readers through the years have felt, a confession of faith, of far greater value to us in revealing "what Paul thought" than in giving a picture of the Roman church and of its particular problems. Actually, some scholars are inclined to see our "Romans" as but one copy of a farewell letter Paul wrote to all his churches in the East, and which he felt would be valuable, with some additions (chap. 15), to ensure him a proper welcome free from suspicions aroused by unwarranted, not to say malicious, reports which Christians in Rome had received about the man who had "turned the world upside down" and was coming there also.

Paul went to a martyr's death, but his influence, like that of the

Lord he so zealously served, did not die with him. Instead it may well have served to add both to his prestige and his authority. "Remember nothing but good of the dead" is no new discovery. Paul's hand had been heavy and his reproofs both severe and cutting. Many had rankled and rebelled. This was past. As the turbulent waters cleared, values often for the moment obscured became more evident.

Nor is this pure conjecture. We have his letters. They had been written to meet definite crises and to answer specific questions. They had not, however, been discarded but had been treasured. That we have all the letters which Paul wrote is most improbable; that during the early years in "the regions of Syria and Cilicia" his work had been essentially different from what it was in the years we know him as a champion of the One he sought to destroy is unlikely. In all likelihood the letter to Laodicea (cf. Colossians 4: 16) has vanished. May he not have written also to the church at Berea? Certainly his first letter to Corinth (1 Corinthians 5: 9) has vanished, save for perhaps one detached page which many believe to be preserved in the collection of parts of letters to the turbulent city on the Isthmus which we style 2 Corinthians.

Collection of the Letters

The point is that several of the letters were preserved, presumably because they were felt to be of real value. They were not filed for the sake of posterity; they were read and re-read in the course of regular church services. Eventually they were collected—all those which could be found—and published. It is very possible that this step was the first in what may be styled "on the way to a canon"—i.e. the list of writings accepted by the Church as Holy Scripture.

What led to this attempt to collect these earlier letters and make them available for all Christians is far from certain. Various and different explanations have been offered. Some have seen this as a consequence of the Book of Acts. One reader, impressed by the story of Paul which occupied so large a part, knew at first hand a letter from the martyred hero. His church still had it. Using the Acts of the Apostles as a sort of ready-reference book, he had visited the churches mentioned in it and had gathered up all of the letters still remaining. Thus it was Acts which brought Paul, long in eclipse, back into prominence.

This view has gained wide acceptance and is far from impossible. It is, of course, guess-work. It is equally possible that the reverse is true. Paul had not gone into eclipse. Instead his martyr's death had but thrown a more intense light upon him. Churches which had known him and which had letters from him were eager for more. It was this informal collecting of his letters and sharing their content which led to a later writer choosing Paul as the illustrative key figure responsible for the wide spread and success of the Gentile mission.

Whatever the precise steps may have been, one fact is sure. By the end of the first century—very probably about ten or twenty years before that date—collections of Paul's letters were known and were being read, presumably in church services. It was not that they were regarded as Scripture, in our phrase, "canonical". Instead, they were being prized because they were of manifest value, and Christians were becoming fond of them.

They had come to set a fashion in Christian circles and speedily they led to more Christian writing in letter form. Students of the New Testament Book of Revelation have been surprised by one very conspicuous difference in this book. In many respects it is not a unique book, as it so often has been regarded. It is but one of many such writings which flourished for about three centuries (165 B.C.–A.D. 125). But unlike its fellows it contains seven "letters to churches" (2: 1–3: 22).

27

That these are transcripts of actual letters sent to these several churches is most unlikely. What, then, led to this strange element appearing in a standard apocalypse? To many students the answer is clear: it is a consequence, a reflection, of Paul's habit of writing letters to his churches. More than this, it would certainly seem to imply that Paul's letters had been collected and were known to this later author as a collection. Nor should it be overlooked that just as there are letters to *seven* churches in this collection, so the letters of Paul were to *seven* churches—Rome, Corinth, Galatia, Ephesus, Philippi, Colossae, and Thessalonica.

More than that, we have *seven* other writings purporting to be letters and written by other apostles: James; 1 and 2 Peter; 1, 2, 3 John; Jude (the so-called Catholic Epistles). That these later "adventures in writing" reflect the earlier Pauline habit would seem indisputable, and the same may be said for the early letters of Ignatius and Polycarp. More important still: all this suggests that the view often expressed that Paul went into eclipse after his death, only subsequently to be cautiously revived, is quite unwarranted. The hesitation which many scholars see in some second-century writers, notably Justin Martyr, to refer too directly to Paul is not to be explained by any obscurity or unpopularity under which Paul was then suffering. On the contrary, it most probably is to be explained by the fact, as will later be emphasized, that Paul was being loudly championed by one Christian leader; a leader feared and hated for his extremely effective heresy. Thus, for the instant, discretion suggested caution in too direct references to the one who was being touted by this dangerous foe.

The so-called Catholic Epistles to which we have just referred are, of course, *epistles*, not letters. As the term "catholic" suggests, they were "general" writings, not intended for any one church but for all Christians everywhere to whom they might chance to come. This very fact would certainly suggest that by the time of their composition the letters of Paul, which not only had made them inevitable but had served as so explicit a pattern, had come to be regarded as the property of—even if not specifically directed to—all Christians everywhere.

Additions to Paul's Collection?

This habit of Paul of keeping in touch with his churches by personal letters had another consequence. Not only did it set the style for early Christian writings and encourage later Christians to adopt this means of communication, but it led to attempts by later Christians to add to the all-valuable Pauline collection of letters. How many of these Paul-like letters were produced is hard to say. Some are so obviously un-Pauline—even un-Paul-*like*—that their nature is transparent. There are others of a far more sober nature, now safely preserved in our New Testament. Many students of the early Christian literature would incline to the view that Ephesians and 2 Thessalonians are so to be regarded; that is, not written by Paul himself, as they claim to be, but by later Christians writing in their revered master's name, and modeling their work upon genuine letters of Paul, namely, Colossians and 1 Thessalonians.

Many Christians have taken unnecessary offense at such appraisals, especially in view of the term *pseudonymous* often used to distinguish the supposed Paul-like from Pauline. It seems to smack of deceit and fraud and to imply that such letters, if the case were to be proved, must be spurious, if not vicious— at any rate unworthy of a place in the New Testament.

All of this concern is quite unnecessary. Present standards of literary ethics which prohibit a man from writing in the guise of another, an historical figure, primarily for the purpose of cashing in on the reputation of the one whose name he improperly assumes, were not the standards of the ancient world. Such a practice was perfectly natural and respectable. Many writings were produced in the name of those long since dead—Adam and Eve, Abraham, Moses, Ezra; to mention but a random few. Some of the writings in the Old Testament, in whole or in part, are of precisely this nature.

The early writers would have been both amazed and shocked at the charge of fraud. They were not trying to masquerade in the guise of the earlier personage, and were certainly utterly free from any desire to make money by such an impersonation. On the contrary, it was the act of the truest humility and piety. Ideas were not personal possessions and property. The all-important question was; were they true? If so, of course the great heroes of the past, to whom God had unburdened Himself in an intimate way befitting their stature, had known these truths. The present writer was but giving expression to what he had learned, was but passing on the torch, was but saying what Abraham or Moses or Ezra would say, were they still alive. Thus, far from being dishonest in writing in the name of the long-dead hero, dishonesty would have been the case had they sought to express as their own what was clearly the product of another. And of course the presence of the earlier name as author would give more certain weight to the all-important truth to be announced.

To the modern man there may well seem one fatal objection; was the confidence warranted, which these writers had in what was to them so certain and so unreservedly true as to guarantee its virtual authorship from the past? To this objection nothing can be said save that it is of a sort never to have occurred to the minds of our early brethren, and that it does not involve in the slightest degree anything of dishonesty or intended deceit.

One more point needs to be stressed. It would seem obvious, but it is too often overlooked. Some years ago a cartoon frequently appeared. An old lady in tears held the empty black covers of the Bible. Above the picture was the caption, "The

Critics Have Taken Away My Bible." To many, aghast at what seemed the sinister work of the "Higher Critics", the artist was right. They failed to see that the picture was not only wrong, but wrongheaded. The contents of the Bible had not been removed. It was still there, still as substantially bound between the covers as it had ever been, and still begging to be read and profited from.

That the Galilean fisherman Peter was the actual author of the two epistles now bearing his name; that James the brother of Jesus was the man who wrote the blunt and vigorous attack upon sham and smug pretence; that Paul was the author of a letter claiming to be addressed to a city in which he had labored for years but which letter so strangely seemed addressed to strangers —these assumptions might be called into question, but the several books had not been "torn from the Bible". They were still there intact and unaltered. Their innate values, if values there were, were quite unlessened, indeed, quite unaffected, unless one assumes that the truth and value of insights are true and valuable only if uttered by a particular individual.

All this is part of a far larger question which the reverent and devoted labor of students of the Bible through the years has made central. It can be crisply stated: Is a thing true because God said it, or have men become convinced that God said it because it has approved itself to the heads and hearts of men through whom God continues to make Himself known? For those to whom this second alternative is the answer many problems are resolved. And among these problems is the fear that, if evidence seems to suggest a different author for a word—or book—in Holy Writ, values long believed in are thereby destroyed.

2

THREE LETTERS TO CHURCHES

"LETTERS TO THE CHURCHES" is a term which can be applied to a large section of the New Testament. By actual count one-third of its pages carry such. To no small degree Paul had been responsible for this first adventure in Christian writing. During his years of missionary travel he had written constantly to churches which he had established and for which he felt a continued responsibility and affection, and many of these letters, though addressed to individual churches and vibrant with concern for their immediate problems, came to be collected and copied and prized by an increasing circle of readers and eventually to serve as models for more "letters to churches", by other teachers who felt they had words which needed to be spoken.

But in these later writings there is a marked difference. The form might be superficially similar to those of Paul; the purpose, not to mention the content, was very different. No longer were they directed to particular groups confronted with problems, often baffling. Instead, they were epistles—"open letters"—and were intended for all Christians to whom they might come, who were in need of the suggestions (advice and warnings) which the writers felt to be necessary.

The "Personal" Channel

Among these later "letters to the churches" three stand out conspicuously. On the surface they are not "epistles" but personal letters. More than that, they are not addressed to all

Christians everywhere, nor even to one local church. Instead they are in the form of personal letters from Paul to two of his long-time friends and assistants, Timothy and Titus, each now in a position of large responsibility—the one at Ephesus, the other in Crete.

To be sure, in our collection of Pauline letters one, unlike all the others, is to an individual friend, Philemon. Its genuineness is not to be questioned, nor is its value. Brief though it is, it reveals once again the basic ethical soundness of Paul; he will not permit himself to keep another's property, useful though the runaway might prove. And despite his own worries and perplexities he has time to write the word which will ensure a kinder and more understanding reception for the now repentant Onesimus.

In the sharpest contrast to this vibrant and self-guaranteeing note stand the three writings which for two centuries and a half have been styled the Pastoral Epistles, because they purport to contain instruction for Timothy and Titus in their pastoral ministry. These men are now responsible for the oversight and control of churches. They are to guard the deposit, the faith which has been entrusted to them; to unmask and refute wicked teachers who have arisen to oppose the God-given truth and to lure Christians alike from the path of moral rectitude and from the true gospel which alone can ensure that men will renounce irreligious and worldly passion; to live sober, upright, and godly lives in this world. By their own sobriety, integrity, and orthodoxy Timothy and Titus are to seek to set the proper examples.

At whatever angle one views these writings this setting is impossible. Timothy and Titus, known to all readers of the Pauline letters as dear friends and faithful lieutenants of Paul, are here utilized as the recipients of the instruction which the author —for all three letters are so intimately connected in structure, phraseology, and purpose as to demand one author, not several—

B
33

feels the churches require. Since he is writing in the name of Paul, convinced that were Paul alive this is what he would have said, it is not surprising that he has adopted the innocent device of personal recipients. Paul's letters were personal. He had not written to "all the churches" but to the one in Corinth, in Philippi, in Thessalonica. Thus to direct letters to an undesignated group would have destroyed the illusion at the start. And after all, Paul had on occasion written to individuals, as the letter to Philemon so clearly proved.

To style the author a "forger" is nonsense. As has been pointed out, he did not write on carefully aged papyrus in the script of the past century, hoping to fool a publisher into thinking that here was a newly discovered screed, hitherto unknown. It is far from impossible that those who first read the resultant writings knew, as we cannot, the author's name. They were accepted for what they were, an honest attempt to give credit where the writer felt credit was due. He owed to Paul, he was sure, all he knew. To modern critics his work may seem not only "un-Pauline" but actually "un-Paul-*like*", for he does not wear easily the armor which in modesty he has put on. Of course he quarried the Pauline epistles which he had long known so intimately, quite unaware that not infrequently the quoted Pauline phrase was as flat in its new setting—and as conspicuously out of place—as it had been pointed and natural in the original.

Thus Timothy, who in these letters—notably 1 Timothy—is the monarchical pastor (bishop) of the churches about Ephesus, is warned to flee youthful lusts, to live decently, and to let no one minimize his position because of his youth. This not too skillful touch surely reflects Paul's earlier words about the then youthful Timothy (1 Corinthians 16: 10f.; cf. 4: 17). That Timothy—at the time of Paul's impending death—knew that Paul had been "appointed a preacher and apostle, a teacher of the Gentiles in faith and truth" would seem likely. But in these letters it is

34

told him portentously and with an insistent "I am telling the truth, I am not lying" (1 Timothy 2: 7).

"Inspired" or "Orthodox"

This is but one example of two Pauline words, pointed in their original setting in the stormy letter to the rebellious Galatians, oddly out of place in a letter to a mature leader who had known and revered him from the days of his conversion. The historic Timothy presumably knew "how one ought to behave in the household of God", and that "the church of the living God" was actually the "pillar and bulwark of the truth" (1 Timothy 3: 15). Many of the recipients of the letter, however, stood in need of this and similar warnings, and it sounded Pauline. In a word, the depicted situation, "Paul to Timothy and Titus", is simply stage setting, by modern standards far from convincing, for the author's honest (if not especially deftly introduced) advice and warning. As one reads these writings, it is clear on every page, as years ago James Denney so aptly remarked, that while Paul was inspired, the writer of the Pastorals was simply orthodox.

Orthodoxy, the undeviating observance of "sound doctrine", which alone can teach "how men ought to behave in the household of God" so as "to live sober, upright, and godly lives in this world", this for our author is essential. Truth is *the* truth which is in accord with true religion or piety ("godliness"). This he is convinced had been entrusted by Paul, who had so consistently taught it, to the many Timothys and Tituses. Thus Timothy is to "guard the deposit" which has been entrusted to him, "rightly handling the word of truth". Titus is to give instruction in what befits sound doctrine. Thus they will be in worthy succession to Paul whose proudest boast was, "I have kept the faith" (2 Timothy 4: 7). Here "faith" is "the faith", "true religion", the "truth", which is to be guarded from contamination by false teachers who are leading Christians astray. In the injunction "Guard the deposit" (1 Timothy 6: 20) is precisely the emphasis in Jude's "Contend for the faith which was once for all delivered to the saints" (Jude 3).

Faith is no longer the eager turning to Christ, the quality of life which the newborn Christ's man finds himself possessing as the consequence of his mystic union with the One who has set him free. For Paul, faith and action are identical. The quality of life which the one *in Christ* must exhibit is of necessity the fruit, the inevitable result, of his death to the old, his birth to the new. God's will has taken hold of the new man, almost without his knowing it, surely not as a reward for his acceptance of it. Thus for Paul faith is not, as it was later to become, the acceptance of dogmas or tradition. Instead, it was a quality of life which disregarded consequences. For later Christians, content to walk in the paths blazed out by the pioneers, faith has become the unquestioning acceptance of traditions which had been handed down; one might almost say it *is* the tradition and as such is the basis for all right living.

A brief summary of the contents of these three little tracts, cast in letter form, will reveal their real nature, "little treatises on elementary church-law, or primitive church-manuals":

1 Timothy

After a brief and formal salutation (1: 1-2) comes an attack upon false teachers (1: 3-7) who are sowing strife and perverting morals contrary to the sound doctrine which had been entrusted to Paul (1: 8-12), who by God's grace had been changed from a persecutor to one faithful to God's service, an example of the divine mercy (1: 13-17). This task is now Timothy's (1: 18-20), who is given instruction having to do with the life and administration of the churches.

Prayer is to be offered by Christians for all men, including "kings and all who are in high position" (2: 1–7). Men, however, are the ones to offer such prayer (2: 8), while women, in accord with their subordinate position, are to perform their proper duties in all modesty (2: 9–15). Next follows an enumeration of the qualities and conduct of bishops (3: 1–7), deacons [and deaconesses?] (3: 8–13), instruction necessary for the good of the churches, entrusted as they are with the divine secret, and which Paul may be delayed in giving in person (3: 14–16). Then once again the attack is resumed on false teachers whom the Spirit foretells will seduce many with their demands for abstinence from marriage and certain foods (4: 1–5). Against all such Timothy is to stand firm (4: 6–10), an example in personal conduct and careful that the proprieties of the church service be observed (4: 11–16).

Then follows a medley of miscellaneous rules, including Timothy's attitudes towards the young and old of both sexes (5: 1–2), especially towards widows (5: 3–16), elders (5: 17–20), his scrupulous responsibility for fairness and his personal probity (5: 21–25), and the responsibilities of masters and slaves (6: 1–2). Then comes the concluding summary: once more a bitter attack on all who teach differently (6: 3–4), especially on those who are commercializing their teaching through love of money (6: 5–10), an earnest admonition to the "man of God" to shun all this and to "keep the commandment unstained and free from reproach" (6: 11–16), a charge to the rich to do good deeds (6: 17–19), and a final injunction to "Timothy" to guard the deposit and stand firm against the godless chatter stemming from false knowledge (6: 20–21a), and the simple benediction, "Grace be with you" (6: 21b).

After the brief salutation (1: 1–2), very similar to that of
1 Timothy, follows a complimentary paragraph, much as in
Paul's earlier letters, in which Timothy is commended for his
unfeigned faith (1: 3–5) and enjoined to rekindle this gift of
God (1: 6) and to show the same endurance as had Paul himself
(1: 7–2: 14). This section is interrupted by a brief mention of
the defection of Phygelus and Hermogenes (1: 15) and of the
former kindness of Onesiphorus (1: 16–18). By "rightly
handling the word of truth" Timothy is to aid in the overthrow
of the false teachers (2: 14–19) and by his own probity and the
gentleness of his reproof of those who err he is to aid in their
"escape from the snare of the devil" (2: 20–26). Evil days are
predicted, with imposture, as in the time of Moses (3: 1–8), but
"their folly will be plain to all" (3: 9). Against them Timothy
is to stand firm, knowing through the experience of Paul himself that suffering is the lot of all (3: 10–17).

After an essential repetition of this basic demand to stand
firm in the face of even worse days sure to come (4: 1–5), in
which Paul will no longer be able to help, for the time of his
departure is at hand (4: 6–8), Timothy is bidden to come to
Paul, forsaken as he is by all save Luke (4: 9–18). The writing
closes with greetings (4: 19–21) and a brief benediction (4: 22).

Titus

This epistle is the shortest of the three, but the salutation is by
far the longest and most elaborate (1: 1–4). Titus is to appoint
"presbyters" of blameless life in Crete (1: 5–6), for the bishop
must be blameless, able to give instruction in sound doctrine and
to confute opponents (1: 7–9), of whom there are many in
Crete (1: 10–16). He is to "teach what befits sound doctrine"

for the guidance of aged men (2 : 1–2), aged women, the aged to instruct the younger (2 : 3–5), younger men (2 : 6), for whom Titus is to be an example (2 : 7–8), and slaves (2 : 9–10), for this is strictly in accord with God's expressed will (2 : 11–15). He is to inculcate obedience to rulers and the desire for good works in place of the sort of vicious life practised before the goodness and loving kindness of God our saviour appeared (3 : 1–8). This is followed by repeated specific instructions for the treatment of the errorists (3 : 9–11). With a brief personal word about his (Paul's) plans, the direction to Titus to do his best to come to him, brief greetings from "all who are with me", the epistle closes with essentially the same benediction as the other two : "Grace be with you all" (3 : 12–15).

Primitive Church Manuals

If we disregard the superficial setting—Paul to Timothy or to Titus—with the personal touches, most frequent in 2 Timothy, which, whatever their origin, are purely decorative and for the purpose of heightening the impression that they are pages from the pen of the martyred Apostle to the Gentiles, the nature of the three tracts is patent. They are primitive church manuals with especial attention to church offices.

Three themes, tightly joined, are consistently present in all three : (1) Hold fast the tradition; (2) Preserve order in the church; (3) There are many unruly men, vain talkers and deceivers, whose mouths must be stopped.

That some particular circumstance was the occasion for the writing of all the tracts and epistles put forth in the name of long-dead heroes of the past would seem too obvious to require argument. It was not simply the desire to write in the name of Paul or Peter or James which led the later teacher to pick up his pen. In each case some situation, to him at least of great moment and

39

danger, had arisen which prompted his words of warning and re-proof. In this crisis he gave expression to the instruction he was convinced the master would have given were his mouth now not stilled by death.

Thus in the case of these letters the situation is clear. The danger which led to this threefold insistence on the strictest orthodoxy of belief and conduct was from opponents constantly under attack for their vicious views, their fables and endless genealogies, their prohibitions of marriage and various foods and drinks, and their unwarranted boast of alone possessing "what is falsely called knowledge (gnosis)."

While it is risky to attempt to name these errorists—Basilides, Valentinus, Marcion—their general nature is clear. They were a part of a flood of speculative thinking which swept the Roman empire during the second and third Christian centuries. Oriental in its origin, with a distinct dualism—God and the world, God and nature, spirit and nature—it was in no small part a protest against the Western idea that the world and the natural order ex-pressed God's being. Instead, they argued, God is not only above the world; He is against the world. The world is not His creation but the product of some inferior principle, whose very inferiority is a perversion of the divine, the Unknown. Man's inner and true self is thus no part of the world, alien as it is to the creator and his domain. Within the world man is yet a stranger. As the world is that which alienates from God, so God is that which alienates and ultimately frees man from the world.

This type of thinking, commonly styled Gnosticism, while held by many of undoubted sincerity, was ideally suited to exploitation by unscrupulous quacks and hucksters. Nowhere was the menace more real than in the matter of morals. Con-tempt by those who had knowledge for all that was material—of course including the fleshly body—led to excesses and the most flagrant perversions. In the second century the effects upon

Christian churches are clearly to be seen. Several of the more influential gnostic leaders passionately claimed to be Christians and were making costly inroads, as the protests and denunciations of such writers as Irenaeus make all too clear.

A Battle Cry Against Heresy

It can scarcely be doubted that it was to oppose this type of thinking and its promoters that our three "letters to the churches" were produced. They are not an attack on abstract error but a flaming battle cry against a dangerous and coherent heresy which was blasphemously claiming a revelation of divine things more profound than those possessed by the Church. Since several of the heretic-leaders actually claimed Paul as their own champion, it was particularly appropriate that these indignant broadsides of protest were leveled against them in the name of Paul himself.

Some scholars have felt that a more exact identification is possible and have seen the writings directed specifically against one man—Marcion. The sweeping denial by Marcion of the Old Testament and all that smacked of Judaism, and his unqualified adoption of Paul as the only true follower of the Christ who had descended from the hitherto Unknown God to "abolish the law and the prophets", posed such a challenge that in consequence individual Christian groups were forced to join hands to combat the common foe. Marcion had rejected the Old Testament and had substituted his own canon of scripture: the letters of Paul, a gospel (presumably the Gospel of Luke), and a writing of his own, styled the Antitheses, in which he attacked the Old Testament, arguing that not only was it contradicted by Christian Scriptures, but that it was in constant contradiction to itself.

This challenge by Marcion—and it was a highly successful one, as the many attacks he and his followers received for three centuries from scandalized orthodox Christians reveal—did two things. It solidified orthodoxy into a united wall of opposition, with a Catholic Church the result. It gave rise to our earliest orthodox canon of New Testament writings. Had Marcion simply substituted his writings for the rejected Old Testament, the answer would have been easy. But instead he had selected the Pauline epistles and one of the gospels, all of which had been slowly but surely gaining Christian favor.

Was it specifically to attack this heretic so shamelessly claiming to be the one true follower of Paul that our writer leveled his broadside in the name of Paul himself? There is much to commend this guess. Marcion's accepted list of Pauline letters contained ten; that is, all except these three. Why did Marcion exclude them? Was it simply because he did not believe them to be from the pen of Paul? Was it because he did not know them? Had they been in existence at the time he made his canon, it is hard to account for his ignorance of them.

Certainly the unmodified statement, "*All* Scripture is inspired by God and profitable for teaching, for reproof, for correction, and for training in righteousness" (2 Timothy 3: 16), is most naturally seen as a blast against Marcion's list. Even clearer is the warning against the "contradictions (literally, 'antitheses') of what is falsely called knowledge" (1 Timothy 6: 20). It is hard to believe that these words were not directed specifically against the work of Marcion precisely so named. If these letters to Timothy and Titus as a whole cannot be seen as directed against and so later than Marcion, this verse must be regarded as a later addition slipped in for that express purpose.

Many scholars however find it impossible to date these letters so late—if directed against Marcion they can scarcely be earlier than A.D. 150—largely because of the apparent familiarity with them displayed by Polycarp, whose writing is commonly dated about A.D. 115. While some of the attacks in our letters would

42

have been very apt if directed against Marcion, there are others that would seem quite irrelevant. The warning against Jewish myths (Titus 1:14) is a case in point, for Marcion rejected all such. Certainly he could scarcely be seen as "desiring to be a teacher of the law" (1 Timothy 1:7). His system had no room or time for "endless genealogies" nor a doctrine of aeons. He did renounce marriage and demand an avoidance of meat and wine, but his morals were of the highest and most rigorous sort.

At best the matter is uncertain. Even if directed against Marcion, it is probable that others, loosely and inexactly joined by the writer with Marcion, are included in this broadside attack. To what extent a more exact identification was impossible is for us at this distance hard to say.

Defense of The Pauline Faith

It would seem wisest not to attempt a more precise identification, nor is it necessary for an adequate understanding of this honest, if at times pedestrian, attack upon those whom the writer so heartily disapproved. That the writings are not earlier than A.D. 100 or much, if any, later than 150 would seem highly probable.

It would appear utterly impossible to hazard more than a bare guess at the place from which they were written. Why the author wrote three epistles instead of one he has not hinted, and it is profitless at this late date to guess. Occasionally attempts have been made to arrange them in order of writing, with some lapse of time between. In these attempts Titus usually occupies the middle position, but equally plausible cases can be made and have been for the resultant two orders: 2 Timothy, Titus, 1 Timothy; 1 Timothy, Titus, 2 Timothy.

While most scholars to-day find it impossible to assign the letters as we have them to Paul, many still incline to see them containing genuine bits of otherwise unpublished Pauline letters, notably such personal bits as the request for the "cloak" and "parchments" (2 Timothy 4: 13) and the mention of the evil done him by Alexander the coppersmith (4: 14). Some have gone so far as to argue that 2 Timothy, in which these touches are most frequent, was the expansion of an unpublished letter of Paul which had come into this later Paulinist's hands and had prompted his epistolary attempts. None of these arguments is to me convincing. Of course the author would desire that his work should sound Paul-like. With Paul's letters before him it would not have been difficult to introduce a phrase here and there to increase the resemblance.

The argument that the personal touches, notably in 2 Timothy, "sound natural" proves nothing. It is a poor writer—and our author definitely was not such—who cannot achieve some success in making his work "sound natural". There would seem to be nothing in these letters not adequately accounted for if we believe that their writer, devoted to the memory of Paul, whose letters he knew but whose thought was often far from known, had attempted to meet a situation which seemed to him of deadly peril for the Christian faith. To this end he wrote as he believed Paul would have done, had he been still alive. And he sought, not always too successfully, to make his writing sound as Paul-like as possible.

PART II

"HOLD FAST THE TRADITION"

3

"HOLD FAST THE TRADITION"

THAT THESE three little letters to Timothy and Titus met a real need is evident in the welcome they received and their instant adoption as part of the Pauline legacy. Nor have they ever lost that appeal.

Brief in extent, naturally placed after all the "other" letters of Paul, save the single-page little gem to Philemon, their sober and down-to-earth common sense, their black-and-white rules for conduct, and their unqualified warnings against those who were seeking to upset and confuse the faithful by false doctrines and vicious conduct have made them perennial favorites.

Play the Man in Dangerous Days

To view them simply as "three more letters of Paul" is not only misleading but goes far to depriving them of their real contribution. Even for many who have become convinced of the impossibility of viewing them as coming from the pen of Paul, the presence of occasional bits of personal detail (especially in 2 Timothy), easily regarded as "Pauline", and the frequent repetition of words and phrases from the earlier letters, have proved misleading. By emphasizing them it is very easy to overlook the real contribution of the nameless author himself. As has already been suggested, these elements, too often made central by modern readers, are but superficial parts of the letters. They were used by the author in his desire to make his writings "sound Pauline", to give the weight of his hero's voice to what he was convinced that voice, long stilled in death, would have said were he still alive. Thus a far wiser approach to these little letters to "Timothy" and "Titus" will disregard—or at least will refrain from making central—these "touches which seem so Pauline". Instead, it will attempt to see through the eyes of this (to us) unnamed second-century churchman writing in passionate concern to his fellow Christians to play the man and to hold fast to the precious truth which they have received and which alone can save them from complete disaster.

Conditions were greatly different in his day from what they had been a century before. Then apostles and other devoted missionaries had sought to be, as they believed their Master had enjoined, fishers of men. To change the figure for another equally well-attested, they had gone out "to the highways and hedges" in the attempt to compel people to come in. And success had crowned their efforts. Many had found the call attractive.

But this success brought many serious problems. In a word, the second-century leaders had to handle the results! Many of those who had come were proving a distinct liability, were of the sort to seem to illustrate the warnings in the gospels about those "who come in sheep's clothing but inwardly are ravenous wolves," who were, as Paul had styled them, "enemies of the cross of Christ". They were making easy converts among many of the well-intentioned but inexperienced and bewildered brethren for whom Christ died. In the early days of the Christian mission a sense of overpowering compulsion—"so much to do, so little time"—that when the Lord returned He would find faith in the earth had been the spring of action. "Woe to me if I do not preach the gospel," not the thought of material gain, had driven Paul—and the many other Pauls who never found a Luke to immortalize their names—over weary miles, with constant hardship and danger.

With the increase in numbers and respectability of the movement this had changed. "Hucksters of the gospel," as Paul had indignantly styled them, had arisen. All too clear is the repeated sounding of warnings, not alone in the reported speech of Paul to the elders at Miletus: "Take heed to yourselves and to all the flock, in which the Holy Spirit has made you guardians, to feed the church of the Lord. . . . I know that after my departure fierce wolves will come in among you, not sparing the flock . . ." (Acts 20: 28f.), but in the revealing word of I John, "Beloved, do not believe every spirit, but test the spirits to see whether they are of God; for many false prophets have gone out into the world" (4: 1). In a word, it had become profitable to be a preacher, and safeguards were becoming necessary. In this connection the down-to-earth common-sense instructions in the *Didache* (chap. 11), roughly of the same date as our Pastorals, may be read and pondered with profit.

The A B C of Morals

It was in this situation that our author wrote. Many in the churches had not learned the A B C of morals, especially sexual morals, demanded of those who would bear the name of Christ, for they had not had a heritage in Judaism where this insistence (though not always observed) was central. Too, they needed instruction and discipline. Without admitting it in so many words, Christians were becoming aware that the return of Christ, earlier believed to be momentarily at hand, was a truth to be cherished and believed in, but less the all-powerful, all-else-eclipsing expectation it had earlier been. Occasional voices to the contrary might still be raised, but the passionate concern was waning. Of course the Lord would return in God's good time. In the meantime life must go on. Leaders in the local churches, too often ill-trained and inexperienced, must be found to guard the sheep from the ever-ready wolves.

To provide help in this time of need our author wrote. The day of the path-breaking pioneers was past. As seems so regularly the case, their successors were content to follow in the trails their predecessors had blazed and to turn them into smooth and well-paved highways. Thus it is very easy—and it has been often and properly done—to style such a writer as our later Paulinist as one far more concerned for orthodoxy than for inspiration, more concerned for specific rules of conduct than for debates about self-expression. Of course it was, in a real sense, a "return to legalism", or at least an emphasis on the need and value of laws. Children, even "babes in Christ", need rules. Paul, our author was profoundly convinced, had seen that need. Now on every hand there seemed a desperate need to meet this situation, to teach men "how one ought to behave in the household of God" (1 Timothy 3 : 15) and to "live sober, upright, and godly lives in this world" (Titus 2 : 12).

This good is to be achieved by a strict adherence to the "truth", that is, the "sound doctrine" which had been entrusted to them from God Himself through those, like Paul, whom He had specially endowed. Farthest from the mind of our author is the desire to add to this truth. Indeed, he who would serve in the cause of God must "hold firm to the sure word as [it has been] taught [by Paul], so that he may be able to give instruction in sound [that is, orthodox] doctrine and also to confute those who contradict it" (Titus 1 : 9).

Ethics and Good Order

Our author is an ethical teacher and administrator, not a theologian, systematic or speculative. His continued and blistering denunciation of false teachers and his characterization of their impious attempts as "godless chatter" is revelatory of the man himself. In no sense is he a creative thinker. Instead he stands in the ranks of those who can affirm: "What was good enough for Moses is good enough for me." It need scarcely be said (1) that in this affirmation he would have substituted "Paul" for "Moses" and (2) that despite his loyalty to Paul he was far from understanding him. What he sought to do was to present Paul's teaching correctly, that is, in strict accord with correct orthodox opinion. This means, of course, that his "correct presentation" of Paul not infrequently reveals the outlook of the author himself far more than it does the Paul he so admires.

Despite his lofty idea of Christ our author is a strict believer in the oneness of God. God is "the blessed and only Sovereign, the King of kings and Lord of lords, who alone has immortality and dwells in unapproachable light, whom no man has ever seen or can see" (1 Timothy 6: 15f.). He is "our Savior, who desires all men to be saved and to come to the knowledge of the truth" (1 Timothy 2: 3f.). No less than six times in these little letters He is so styled. To a degree this may seem to lessen the width of the gulf between man and this Mighty and Altogether Other; it does it only in part. One cannot read these writings without feeling that God's majesty has made Him remote in a way very different from that of the preceding century. To be sure, the title Father for God occurs in each of the epistles but never as a term expressing the author's own concept. It stands in the conclusion of the three introductory greetings, taken over bodily from Paul's own style of composition: "Grace, mercy, and peace from God the Father and Christ Jesus our Lord" (1 Timothy 1: 2; 2 Timothy 1: 2). The "fatherhood of God", to whom there is always ready and immediate access—one of Christianity's often unacknowledged debts to Jewish Law, and evident on nearly every page of Paul's letters—is not to be discovered in these pages.

Instead, "there is one God, and there is one mediator between God and men, the man Christ Jesus" (1 Timothy 2: 5), who through giving Himself as a ransom removed the barrier. But our author is not concerned with the nature of the barrier thus removed, the one to whom the ransom is paid, or the reason for its efficacy. Nor does he develop, as his theologically-minded successors were to do, the weighty implications of this once used word "mediator".

His idea of Christ is similarly high. Without deliberately attempting it, he has set a wide gulf between Christ and man. The mystic communion with Christ, so fundamental to the thinking of Paul, and expressed in the all-central phrase "in Christ", is quite absent. Every trace of subordination of Christ to God has gone. No longer is He God's "servant". Even the familiar designation, "God's son", has disappeared. Four times He is styled savior (2 Timothy 1: 10; Titus 1: 4; 2: 13; 3: 6); once quite plainly "our great God and Savior" (Titus 2: 13). It may well be that this latter phrase, which has so worried translators, is here a part of a quotation rather than a phrase coined by our author. At any rate, it apparently appeared to him entirely proper. Christ existed "ages ago"—literally "before times eternal"—(2 Timothy 1: 9). His "appearing", both when He became incarnate (2 Timothy 1: 10) and at the end, when He will reappear to judge the living and the dead (2 Timothy 4: 1), are divine "epiphanies", that is, "theophanies", a showing forth of God. Eleswhere in the New Testament the term used for the return of Christ is *parousia*. This term does not occur in the Pastorals. Instead he regularly uses *epiphaneia*, which, aside from 2 Thessalonians 2: 8, where it is joined with *parousia*, is not found elsewhere in the New Testament. It may well be that the use of the term—otherwise, as is true of *parousia*, used only of the "Second Coming"—to indicate the incarnation is a deliberate Christian protest against the pagan practice of thus designating the birthday of the emperor, that is, the time when "the god appeared".

One marked contrast between the thinking of Paul and that of his later admirer is found in the number of times they refer to Spirit or Holy Spirit. In the Pauline letters it is a very common term, occurring at least eighty times—ninety for those who regard Ephesians as Pauline. In the Pastorals it occurs but three times, twice in apparent quotations (2 Timothy 1: 14; Titus 3: 5), once in a more general reference to an earlier prophecy: "Now the Spirit expressly says that in later times some will depart from the faith . . ." (1 Timothy 4: 1). While no cautious interpreter of Paul would style him as a "trinitarian" (preacher of the Trinity) or even a "tritheist" (preacher of three Gods), his stress upon the Spirit is such as to make possible, if not inevitable, the later dogma. In sharp contrast, in the thinking of our author the concept, as well as the term, is of little or no consequence.

Probably it is fair to say that there is no real confusion between God and Christ in the thought of our author. It is God who has done what has been done; Titus 3: 4–6 may in this connection be cited. But the almost casual way in which now one, now the other, is styled "our Savior" leaves little room for doubt that in the extremely practical—and conspicuously non-theological—thinking of our author Christ has come to occupy a place which renders the term "ditheism" (belief in two Gods) scarcely an exaggeration.

Piety and Good Works

As has been earlier remarked, "faith" for our author is poles apart from what it meant to Paul. No longer is it a way of life, the way a man becomes identified with Christ. Instead, it is loyalty or adherence to certain religious beliefs, which a man can deny (1 Timothy 5: 8) and which Paul can be praised as having "kept" (2 Timothy 4: 7), In its place stands *piety*, a word never

53

used by Paul but which occurs (with its related verb and adverb) no less than thirteen times in these epistles. Upon his piety and good works a man's salvation depends. This clear evidence that for our second-century writer Christianity has hardened into a system of beliefs is confirmed by the comparison of two basic passages: "For those whom he foreknew he also predestined to be conformed to the image of his Son, in order that he might be the first-born among many brethren. And those whom he predestined he also called; and those whom he called he also justified, and those whom he justified he also glorified" (Romans 8 : 29f.). So Paul: the *believer* is foreordained to salvation. "Fight the good fight of the faith; take hold of the eternal life to which you were called when you made the good confession in the presence of many witnesses" (1 Timothy 6 : 12). So our author: *salvation* is foreordained to the believer. This is far from a trivial or accidental variation which the same man might easily make in discussing the same subject. Rather, it shows a fundamental difference of outlook.

From the earliest days baptism had had an essential role in the Christian movement. Apparently an outgrowth of proselyte baptism, required by Judaism of all who would become Jews, it had in the course of the years become a life-giving sacrament (cf. John 3 : 5). That by the end of the first century this stage had been reached is clear in the reference in 1 Peter 3 : 20–21 to the eight persons who were "saved through water which also after a true likeness doth now save you, even baptism" (English Revised Version). That Paul believed, as the author of 1 Peter manifestly did, in baptismal regeneration is perhaps unlikely, although it is sure that in his eyes it was far more than an act of outward obedience in testimony to an inward change which had already taken place. By baptism the person admitted was brought into mystic union with the risen Lord, shared in this death and resurrection, and was thus born anew.

For our author baptism had been for many years the means of entrance into the church, and he takes it for granted as indispensable for salvation. We have no statement in his own words as to its precise relation to "faith", that is, to the acceptance of Christian doctrine; but we have his wholehearted endorsement—"the saying is true"—to what would seem a stanza from a baptismal hymn:

> By a washing that gave us a new birth
> And by making us new through the Holy Spirit,
>   Which he poured on us richly
>   Through Jesus Christ our Saviour;
> That being justified by his grace
>   We might await with firm hope
> An inheritance of eternal life   (Titus 3 : 5-7—Easton).

Such an endorsement leaves little question that he shares the common view of his day. The act of baptism is of itself efficacious. Dying with Christ, which was the real meaning of baptism, has fallen out of sight. Baptism is little more than a purifying rite, the way, as he phrases his introduction to the quoted stanza, "he (that is, God) saved us."

The Place of Baptism

At once a question arises. When did baptism take place? In Pauline churches, and certainly the same situation is evident in the stories in Acts (2: 41; 8: 12f., 38: 10: 48; 16: 33; 22: 16), baptism followed immediately upon profession of faith as the natural consequence of it. By the beginning of the third century the practice had become quite different. A long period of instruction and probation must intervene between the candidate's profession of faith and his admittance to the all-important saving rite. During this period his worthiness was under constant scrutiny and test, and the genuineness of his faith must be evidenced by his manner of life, that is, by his "good works". During this time he was excluded from the Christian meal, for he was not as yet saved. In fact, despite his profession of faith and his evidence of its genuineness in his resulting manner of life, should he die before the actual baptism his salvation was far from certain—apparently in many eyes quite unlikely—save in the one case of martyrdom. Should he die as a martyr, before finishing his instruction period and thus before baptism, he would certainly be saved, for then he would truly have been baptized in his own shed blood. Certainly Justin Martyr's revealing account of the way converts received this all-important "washing with water" (*Apology* i, 61) suggests that by the middle of the second century there had come to be an interval between the time when the convert was first "persuaded and believed that what we teach and say is true" and the moment he was "brought by us where there is water" and was "regenerated in the same manner in which we were ourselves regenerated." And this intervening period was a time of prayer and fasting.

Our author was not writing, as was Justin, a defence to non-Christians for Christian life and practice, in which descriptions were to be expected; nor was he writing for a later age which might be interested in earlier practice. Instead he was writing to fellow Christians as well informed as was he in contemporary practice, even though they needed definite encouragement to make their lives conform. In a word, he was writing to make saints, not historians. Thus with many questions, which we would like answered, he is quite unconcerned.

In passing, it may be commented that there is no slightest allusion to the Lord's Supper, which certainly had been for many years a central part of Christian worship. This (to us) strange omission certainly does not suggest that he minimized its importance. For one to whom true piety consisted so definitely in holding fast, that is, scrupulously observing the traditions, a question at this point is unthinkable. It is simply another indication that his attempt was severely practical—to protest and warn against dangers and perversion, not to produce an all-complete handbook. It may be inferred from his silence at this point that the earlier abuses of this sacred meal, which had so greatly worried Paul (1 Corinthians 11: 17–34), no longer existed. The much-quoted—and debated!—words: "No longer drink only water, but use a little wine for the sake of your stomach and your frequent ailments" (1 Timothy 5: 23) are scarcely to be seen as "definitely medical advice against total abstinence." That such use was made of wine in our author's day is well attested, but with the rejection of the claim of the letter to be the word of Paul to Timothy the force of the personal advice is certainly lessened and the probability increased that here we have a definite attack upon a formal practice, in addition to an incidental indication of the writer's own middle-of-the-road type of ethics, to which severe bodily discipline of any sort was unacceptable. In a word, this may well be a direct protest against the specific ascetic practice of substituting water for the wine of the Lord's Supper, demanded by the false teachers against whom his writing is in no small measure directed. Save for this possible instance, there is no reference to the sacred meal.

Thus it is scarcely surprising that our author's almost casual references to baptism are such as to leave unanswered the question as to the precise moment when the convert is to receive the sacred washing. In absence of direct evidence to the contrary we are probably right in thinking that essentially the same situation may be presumed as comes out in the more direct statement of his contemporary, Justin. Surely his own seeming endorsement of the theology expressed in the baptismal hymn which he quoted would suggest that in his eyes baptism is in and of itself efficacious, the way in which the mercy of an all-powerful God is extended to man. In a word, the church of our author is well on the way towards what may be styled a "magical estimate of baptism" as in reality a life-giving sacrament.

The Practical Teacher

This should not obscure the fact that our author is a definitely practical (non-theological) teacher. We are chosen and saved, not on the basis of any merits of our own but in accord with His own gracious purpose by God: "who saved us and called us with a high calling, not in virtue of our works but in virtue of his own purpose and the grace which he gave us in Christ Jesus ages ago" (2 Timothy 1: 9). Nonetheless, as his letters make very clear, this is far from automatic. Christians have very definite responsibilities: they have been saved by God, but they must nonetheless save themselves through proper conduct, impossible except in consequence of their correct belief: "Take heed to yourself and to your teaching; hold to that, for by so doing you will save both yourself and your hearers" (1 Timothy 4: 16).

At this point a real difference between Paul and his later champion is to be seen, although it is somewhat obscured by the latter's use of his idol's words. For Paul faith and action are inseparable, for faith is not acceptance of beliefs but actually a quality of life, the new life of the newborn Christian. Thus this new life which the Christian lives since he is now "in Christ" is in soberest fact the "fruit" of the Spirit. In theory it is not his

58

choice; rather it is inevitable, the way he must live in consequence of his new birth. Should he fail, it simply goes to show that he is not "in Christ," has not been born anew. Else he could not fail to bear the fruits, for if the root is holy, so must be the branches.

For the later writer there is a difference. The faith which he must embrace, that is, the deposit which he must guard, the tradition which he must uphold, is not the root, but the foundation upon which he stands: "the pillar and bulwark" which support him and apart from which he cannot hope to stand. Upon this sure foundation he can preserve and accomplish the good works which will be recognized and rewarded at Christ's appearance.

The difference is real and should not be overlooked. On the other hand it should not be overstressed. To be sure, for Paul the new man finds himself borne on by the Spirit, with the old hostility, so unforgettably phrased in the seventh chapter of Romans, past. No longer is he kicking in vain against the goads. Instead, he is at peace with God, loving the things which God loves (Romans 5: 1). Unfortunately all around him Paul found the sad reverse, and his greatest contribution lies in his vigorous and direct insistence that these new men give proof of it in their lives. In theory there would be no place for his ethical demands, his warnings and rebukes. And many of his converts so believed and protested. They were "in Christ," had received the Spirit, even as he had. Why then should he seek to direct and lord it over them? In one breath he was teaching them they were "free from the law," had died to the old bondage; in the next he was sounding precisely the same do's and don'ts as had the Law, and was insisting that the demanded course of life was alone "worthy of one in Christ".

Paul never reconciled the two. The nearest he could so do was to consider his erring converts only "babes in Christ" and in constant need of his admonitions and oversight. Thus while in theory the course of life which they would live was inevitable, in practice he spent his strength in striving to make them achieve what in theory should have been automatic.

On the basis of his theology he could insist that Christian action must and does result directly from the Spirit and could sum up this confidence: "Whatever does not proceed from faith is sin" (Romans 14: 23). Nonetheless he could and did insist that they "work out [their] own salvation with fear and trembling" (Philippians 2: 12). To be sure, the desired results were "fruits of the Spirit"; nevertheless many of his converts felt, and rightly, that they must be very zealous and active farmers or fruitgrowers.

For our author this problem simply does not exist. In his practical down-to-earth thinking this "Spirit guidance" plays no part. On occasion he may use the term, for it is part of the words and phrases he had inherited, but it does not express his outlook. The problem faced by Paul, that freedom could easily degenerate into licence, and contempt of good works into contempt for proper conduct, was no problem for our author. He has no fear of good works. In all three of the epistles he repeatedly insists upon their necessity. By "doing good," "being rich in good deeds", Christians "lay up for themselves a good foundation for the future, so that they may take hold of the life which is life indeed" (1 Timothy 6: 18). This particular quotation is from his word to those "rich in this world", but it is at once evident from his constant insistence that it is equally true of every other Christian. It is not that by independent doing of these good works a man merits and can demand from God salvation. This to our author would be unthinkable. Of course, salvation is the free gift of God; but in accepting this gift he allows without theological anxiety for a very real and important co-operation on the part of man.

It is no exaggeration to say that our author's object is primarily concerned with conduct. His basic concern is that men may "live sober, upright, and godly lives in this world". Only so may they have any ground for belief that they will share in the coming triumph: "our blessed hope, the appearing of the glory of our great God and Savior Jesus Christ" (Titus 2: 13). And no clearer picture of what may be styled his "Christian ethics" is to be found than in Titus 2, from which these two quotations are made.

Thoughtful reading of this chapter, which might be aptly styled "out of my life and thought", reveals the basic qualities and attitudes of the truly religious man and woman. Particular virtues are here stressed for the several groups in the church— older men, older women, young women, younger men, the teacher (bishop?) himself, slaves—and may be considered in more detail in connection with his view regarding right organization. They are nonetheless a fair picture of "what befits sound doctrine." Nor is it an undue simplification to say that his standard is what is seemly, prudent, useful, and above all in accord with accepted custom.

His list of virtues starts with a familiar Greek trio: temperance, gravity, and self-control. To this is coupled a Christian trio, faith, love, and steadfastness. For Paul love had been central, "the fulfilling of the law" (Romans 13: 10). Not so to our author. Such an utterance would be unthinkable, as would be the almost lyric description of this all-central virtue, so pathetically lacking in many of his converts in the city on the Isthmus (1 Corinthians 13). Without doubt our author knew this section, as he did all of the apostle's writing. It is equally certain that he did not accord it the all-else-eclipsing place it has come to occupy in the thinking of many. He uses the word *love* ten times in his letters, but it never stands alone; it is regularly joined with some other quality as steadfastness, self-control, fidelity, piety, prudence. The related verb occurs but twice (2 Timothy 4: 8, 10), and in the latter of the two occurrences is used of Demas's desertion of Paul, for he had "loved" this present world. This conspicuous difference, not alone of vocabulary but of outlook, is but one of the many indications of the later disciple who, while a devoted Paulinist, was far from being a Paul.

The other adjectives in this sample passage—reverent in behavior, no slaves to drink, loving their husbands and children, chaste, domestic, submissive to their husbands, grave, of sound (correct, orthodox) speech, unrefractory, obedient, free from worldly passion—complete the picture. It is easy to style it pedestrian, even a middle-of-the-road sort of ethic where moderation is near compromise. Rather, it would seem to be fairer to style it down-to-earth common sense in essential agreement with what had for centuries been the Greek ideal, the golden mean: "in nothing too much".

He is uncompromising in his disapproval of extreme bodily self-denial in all its forms. The good things of life are to be enjoyed, not shunned. Chastity, yes; celibacy, no. Regularly in his words about those who would be leaders in the church is the insistence that they be "the husband of one wife". Only as a man knows how to rule his own family can he be expected to know how to rule the church. Similarly there is no ban on foods or wines. Moderation, yes indeed, drunkenness and its consequent excesses are repeatedly deplored; but attempts to insist upon abstinence from what God has created to be received with thanksgiving are to be avoided, "for everything created by God is good" (1 Timothy 4: 1–5). In a word, "To the pure all things are pure" (Titus 1: 15). So in the case of money. The love of and straining after wealth is repeatedly condemned, but if a man has property he is expected to use it properly and for good purposes—of which there are many (cf. 1 Timothy 6: 17ff.).

Moderation in All Things

Dignity, the avoidance of everything unseemly in speech and conduct—these are constantly stressed and amplified. Women are to dress modestly and simply and to behave properly "as befits women who profess religion" (1 Timothy 2: 10). Under no circumstance is she to attempt the overthrow of what is seemly: she is to "learn in silence with all submissiveness. I permit no woman to teach or to have authority over men; she is to keep silent" (1 Timothy 2: 11f.).

As has already been suggested, and as will be amplified later, one of the principal spurs to these insistences was the presence of "false teachers", long ago prophesied by Paul but now in their midst, whose teachings and actions were in flagrant violation of sound doctrine and its resultant conduct. The excesses of Gnosticism had brought about a very definite fear of all that savored of excess. There was as great a danger from being "filled with the Spirit" as there was in being filled with wine. Against all such conduct, everything that smacked of fanaticism or disregard for what was seemly and proper, the writer protests, confident that it is in sorry violation of the sound, that is, long-accepted, doctrine which Christians must of necessity hold fast.

His demands may seem—and in reality were—moderate. Even upon those in especial places of authority, the "Timothys" and "Tituses", the demands were not unreasonable, far from impossible. Yet it is by no means fair to style it an "easy morality". Throughout the epistles is a constant demand: Accept your share of the gospel's hardships (2 Timothy 1: 8). The Christian is to "fight the good fight of the faith" (1 Timothy 6: 12), where both the words selected and the context suggest the picture of the athlete contending in the games, and to "wage the good warfare" (1: 18), where the picture is of the soldier. Neither of these figures of speech—the Christian an athlete contending in the games and the soldier involved in active warfare—was, of course, a new invention of the author. Paul had constantly employed both, and they had become favorites in the vocabulary of Christians. A "soldier of Christ" early became as common a designation for the true believer as its equivalent, "Christian"; nor through the years has it lost its appeal, as Sabine Baring-Gould's beloved hymn attests (*Onward, Christian Soldiers*).

The Steadfast Soldier

But they are more than pure literary flourishes for our author. Rather, they give expression to his insistence upon such unspectacular qualities as steadfastness, endurance, strict adherence to the rules—the requirement laid upon every athlete (2 Timothy 2: 5). Every man who seeks to live religiously must expect to be persecuted, as had been so manifestly true for Paul, must be ready to stand firm under pressure. Nor is this a passive and defensive readiness to endure suffering solely to avoid something worse. Instead, it is a constant and valiant offensive, an unending struggle with temptation and the other enemies of the good life, not a withdrawal from the battle or attempt at escape from duties and obligations for fear of failure and resulting penalties. These qualities and ideals, and the rules for conduct in which they find constant expression, are far from spectacular. To some they have seemed pedestrian, scarcely of the sort to produce saints or to attract, by their seeming impossibility, those eager to mount up on wings as eagles. They were of the sort to encourage men to walk and not faint.

Throughout these epistles there is a conspicuous absence of any interest in or attempt to encourage others to martyrdom or its kindred excesses. Not for him the tireless effort of the fanatic Ignatius to force reluctant Roman officers to crown him with martyrdom and the almost morbid fear lest his friends, led astray by misinformed kindness, prevent him from achieving the goal, now within his reach, of being "ground by the teeth of wild beasts that he may be found pure bread of Christ" (Ignatius, *Romans* 4: 1). Nor are the Timothys and Tituses, young or old, to whom he writes to escape the lures of the flesh by self-mutilation as the youth in Alexandria, mentioned by Justin Martyr (*Apology* i, 29), sought in vain to do and as an Origen accomplished.

For our author all such fanatic desires and antics would have been abhorrent in the extreme. Rather, they are to be husbands of one wife, governing their households with dignity and sobriety, meeting their responsibilities and proving worthy, not shirking them by arrogantly styling as wicked and perverse what God had created and blessed for man's use and profit. Paul is his hero; ever is the master before his eyes. It is his conduct, and that includes his persecutions and sufferings at Antioch and Iconium and Lystra, which the Timothys are to observe and emulate. Nonetheless it may be seriously questioned that he ever found himself in the "strait betwixt the two" (Philippians 1: 22ff., English Revised Version)—or could imagine the dilemma for those to whom he wrote—hard pressed between the desire to "depart and be with Christ" or to remain and continue to strive to be a workman who has no need to be ashamed. In God's own good time the day would come when the Lord would return and would award crowns of righteousness "to all who have loved his appearing" (2 Timothy 4: 8), but the Christian is not the one who sets the day or is to seek to anticipate it.

A century after our author, in the days of Decius, definite and deliberate attempts were to be made to root Christians from the earth, and many soldiers of Christ died for the faith they would not renounce. "Making the good confession" came to have a very different meaning than that which it has for our author. When he writes to Timothy, "Fight the good fight of the faith; take hold of the eternal life to which you were called *when you made the good confession in the presence of many witnesses*" (1 Timothy 6: 12), thoughts of martyrdom are farthest from his mind. The reference is, of course, to baptism, at which time the "Timothys" made their confession "Jesus is Lord," promising to embark on a course of life properly styled "the good fight". As the years wore on, baptism might become a mere formality, though a very necessary one. It was still for our author— although, as we have seen, it was far from what it had meant to Paul—an act of high resolve, essentially like the athlete's pledge to play the game in faithful compliance with the rules. Thus he was a true disciple of his Lord who, unabashed, had made His "good confession" in simple fortitude before Pontius Pilate.

Proper conduct, the ability to show oneself approved, a workman who does not need to be ashamed, is possible only to the man who stands on the one foundation which is secure, namely, correct beliefs which he accepts wholeheartedly and without reservation. It was God's revelation and as such is to be reverenced and faithfully accepted. It had been committed to Paul as a sacred and precious trust and is to be transmitted by a series of approved teachers, who recognize and obey the word of their master. He had fought the good fight, had finished the course, and had kept the faith. His word to those who were to follow after him, the many Timothys and Tituses and all whom they would teach and guide, was clear and without possibility of misunderstanding: Guard the deposit; hold fast the tradition.

4

"PRESERVE ORDER IN THE CHURCH"

THESE LITTLE letters have been styled, and properly, "primitive church manuals with particular reference to church officers". Bishops, elders, deacons, widows receive words of instruction. All this is very different from the situation seemingly evident in the Pauline letters.

That in Paul's churches there were leaders with individual responsibilities is certain. To the Thessalonians he wrote: "But we beseech you, brethren, to respect those who labor among you and are over you in the Lord and admonish you, and to esteem them very highly in love because of their work" (1 Thessalonians 5: 12f.). Similarly the Corinthians are directed to be subject to such men as Stephanas and to give them proper recognition (1 Corinthians 16: 15–18). In his salutation to the "saints in Christ Jesus who are at Philippi" he mentions also "the bishops and deacons". Here alone in his letters are such officers specified. Unless the words are a later addition, which seems improbable, they would seem to mean simply "overseers and assistants", in a word, "those who labor among you and are over you". In his letters to his churches he writes to the individual Christians directly, with no hint of the presence of what may be styled a "clergy". Instead, they are, so to speak, lay churches. Itinerant missionaries, apostles and prophets, not local pastors, are the guides and teachers. It was due to the gift of the Spirit, not to selection and ordination, that apostles, prophets, teachers, workers of miracles, healers, helpers, administrators, and speakers in tongues stood out in the churches (1 Corinthians 12: 28).

The situation in our three letters is thus very different. A far more settled order has been achieved. The church is no longer recruited from the spiritually gifted. Due in part to the lapse of years, the delay in the return of the Lord, and the death of the apostles, the office of prophet was declining. In addition, the advent of false prophets—both hucksters of the gospel, as Paul contemptuously dismissed those whose message was dictated by the hopes of fees and gratuities, and of those who were making heretical inroads into the received tradition—had tended to make the prophetic ministry suspect. The natural result was an attempt to bring the prophets under control. Nor is this situation anything new or novel. Farthest from the thought of the author is the desire to make an innovation. Here as elsewhere his theme is "Guard the tradition." His remark that everybody knows that the office of bishop is a "noble task" (1 Timothy 3 : 1), which is apparently what he means by "a sure saying", is enough to discourage the thought that he is attempting a new ecclesiastical organization. Nor is he attempting, under the shield of Paul's authority, to defend an ecclesiastical organization as had the earlier Ignatius. He takes it for granted. His one interest is that the bishops be good ones, that is, of exemplary life.

Thus many questions which are natural to us to-day find no answer. Is the bishop to be differentiated from the elders (presbyters) "who rule well"? (1 Timothy 5 : 17). Is it a simple accident that in the two passages where the word "bishop" (*episkopos*) occurs (1 Timothy 3 : 2; Titus 1 : 7) it is in the singular, while "elders" (*presbuteroi*), when mentioned as officers (1 Timothy 5 : 17; Titus 1 : 5), not as "older men", only occurs as a plural? Certainly there is no slightest hint, if the two offices are different, of their relationship the one to the other. Once again the modern reader, who would like answers to his questions, is forced to recognize that his questions were not theirs. The author was not writing for a future generation who might like information as to the earlier situation; he was writing to his own generation for whom there was no question at all. His one concern was that in the filling of these offices only men and women of sobriety and of impeccable reputation be had.

The fact that our author has used the setting "Paul to Timothy" and "Paul to Titus" for his words of advice and warning to fellow Christians has heightened the difficulty for the modern reader. Even with the recognition that "Paul to Timothy" and "Paul to Titus" are historically most unlikely it is easy to view these letters as written to church dignitaries—to "Timothy," a settled archbishop of Ephesus; to "Titus", a sort of missionary bishop in the heretofore unorganized territory of Crete. More than that, it has seemed easy to picture the author as himself occupying a position still more elevated on the ecclesiastical ladder. All of this is most uncertain, if not actually improbable.

Letters of a Pastor

The letters would seem to be "open letters" to churches by one who was, so to speak, a pastor. That there was a secure and orderly organization is patent from the instructions in the letters themselves, where it is taken for granted that there are bishops and/or elders, deacons, and widows. As has been constantly stressed, the author is seeking to do what he is convinced Paul would have done were he still alive. Thus the very pertinent query arises: What more natural form of address could he have employed? His readers are "all Christians everywhere". How should he address them? To have limited his address to one church, Ephesus or some other specific group, would have seemingly limited its value. The selection of Timothy and Titus, earlier helpers of Paul, men, like Paul himself, not limited to any one church, would appear to have been a very deliberate choice by our author of what seemed a most natural and Paul-like approach. And it was made the more natural by the fact that Paul on at least one occasion had written to an individual, Philemon.

Frank recognition of this probability enables the modern reader to view the author's concern. He is not interested in justifying, not to mention innovating, an ecclesiastical organization. His one concern is that the men and women in those positions be worthy and well-qualified to promote the gospel as they have received it and to defend it against the false teachers who were seeking to spoil the flock, as Paul had so clearly foreseen.

In addition to the constant admonition to "Timothy" and to "Titus", both as to their responsibilities for direction and their quality of personal life, and which would seem indications of what our author deemed necessary in a church leader, there is an explicit paragraph in 1 Timothy (3 : 1–7) devoted to the bishop. Later in the same epistle (5 : 17–22) is a paragraph devoted to "elders who rule well". That no specific qualifications for them are listed has led many to argue that the "bishop" is but one of this group, that is, that each church now has a group of elders or bishops, responsible for various duties, among which preaching and teaching are specifically listed as especially meritorious. In the opening paragraph of the Epistle to Titus is the admonition to appoint elders in every town (1 : 5–6). Qualities which mark out a man as worthy for the office are the same as those for the bishop in 1 Timothy. In addition, in the next verse (Titus 1 : 7) the author continues: "For a bishop, as God's steward, must be blameless. . . ." This certainly would seem to indicate no change of subject and that the reference to "a bishop" does not mean a sudden mention of a different office but is simply a continuation, that is, "a man who occupies this office (an 'elder') is to be a man of the following qualities".

Nonetheless the fact that in 1 Timothy 3 this particular office is listed first and that the holder of it is mentioned in the singular, in contradistinction to the others, such as deacons and widows, makes it perhaps a bit more probable that by our author's time the bishop was no longer simply one of the "presbytery" but was in a position earlier so heatedly demanded by Ignatius. Certainly this is the case in the roughly contemporary *Didache*, where bishops and deacons "also minister to you the ministry of prophets and teachers" (*Didache* 15 : 1–2).

Our author is not attempting a book of rules, defining each position and specifying the precise function. The fact that he seems to regard the position of bishop as self-explanatory may well indicate that in the lapse of time since Ignatius the matter has been settled and the battle won. These conclusions are at best uncertain and many scholars read the evidence differently.

Qualities for a Bishop

The qualities requisite for a "bishop" indicate the sober, common-sense, middle-of-the-road outlook of our author. He must be "above reproach, married only once, temperate, sensible, dignified, hospitable, an apt teacher, no drunkard, not violent but gentle, not quarrelsome, and no lover of money" (1 Timothy 3 : 1–3). Most of these requirements are self-explanatory and would seem to be required in our author's view of all Christians. The term "married only once" (lit. the "husband of one wife") would certainly suggest—although it may not demand—that he be a married man. Certainly it is not to be taken as a protest against polygamy, the practice of having

71

several wives, which was not permitted in civilized Roman society, not to mention Christian circles. Presumably it did exclude those who were remarried, either after the death of a former wife or in consequence of divorce. Nor was this requirement needless, as the abundant evidence for plurality of marriage, then as now, makes clear. The down-to-earth demand that he "must manage his own household well, keeping his children submissive and respectful in every way; for if a man does not know how to manage his own household, how can he care for God's church?" indicates that celibacy of the clergy had not yet been dreamed.

Throughout these qualifications is the note on moderation: in nothing too much. He must be "temperate", that is, in control of himself. He must not be a drunkard—an injunction for all Christian workers—but there is no demand for total abstinence or other ascetic practices. The repeated injunction against overindulgence in wine would certainly suggest that abuses were far from unknown.

In addition, the repeated injunction against being a "lover of money" or "greedy for gain" would seem to indicate that in the writer's experience such a warning is not superfluous. Whether it is to be looked upon as an indication that among their duties was the collection and supervision of church finances is far from certain, although presumably that had become one of the functions of deacons. Apparently those whose time was largely engaged in Christian duties, especially "preaching and teaching", were to be provided for financially, although there is no direct reference to salaries or other emoluments for officers. "Love of money" is, of course, the root of all evils (1 Timothy 6: 10). Here the author quotes with approval a well-known proverb. For the Christian to harbor such a hankering is fatal and leads to spiritual ruin, as conspicuous examples prove. But money itself is no evil, and when properly handled may well be a blessing, both for those who are aided and for those who thus have the means to be rich in good deeds.

Fear of money and suspicion of those who have it, so conspicuous in the gospels, has long since passed. No longer is the church recruited alone from the poor and the lowly. Men of property are no longer feared. Our author's outlook is essentially that of the author of the *Shepherd of Hermas*, who can compare the rich with the elm tree which supports and aids the vine (the poor) to greater fruit, or of Clement of Alexandria, who sees in the gospel story of the stark word to the Rich Ruler, "Sell all that you have," a dark parable requiring much interpretation.

Nor is it to be overlooked that these officers are to be mature as Christians, as well as in years. Deacons are to be tested: only after they have proved themselves are they to serve (1 Timothy 3: 10). The bishop is "not to be a recent convert", lest he be "puffed up with conceit" (1 Timothy 3: 6). This qualification, it may be observed in passing, would indicate a far later day than Paul's, whose churches, of necessity, were all composed of "recent converts".

Rules for Women

The solid, homely, common-sense sobriety of the author is conspicuous in his rules and qualifications for women. Whether the churches of his day had deaconesses who bore that title is uncertain. Certainly the function later assigned to such would seem to be that of the enrolled widows listed in 1 Timothy 5: 3–16. Amid the qualifications of deacons stands a verse which has caused much difference of opinion: "The women likewise must be serious, no slanderers, but temperate, faithful in all things" (1 Timothy 3: 11). The colorless noun "women" may signify "female deacon", but more probably is to be understood as

73

"their wives". Because a deacon's wife would of necessity be far more closely associated with her husband's work than would the wife of a bishop, it is not surprising that their reliability and freedom from tale-bearing were stressed.

In his long and careful description of the qualifications of the group which he styles "real widows" (1 Timothy 5: 9–16)—in the King James (Authorized) Version "widows indeed"—the author not only gives several hints of abuses which must be guarded against but of his own very realistic down-to-earth and practical ethics. To be enrolled as a widow, that is, a recognized assistant, a woman must not only be a widow who has been married but once but she must be at least sixty years of age. Younger widows are not to be enrolled lest they marry again. Not only that, younger women are apt to be idlers, gadding about from house to house, spreading gossip, and proving a menace to sobriety and good order. In his fear that they "grow wanton against Christ and desire to remarry" is not to be seen any self-denying or straitlaced hostility to marriage, even to re-marriage. Instead, that is what he counsels these younger widows to do, namely, remarry, bear children, and act as women should.

In the case of those of maturer years, their past reputation for good deeds, their successful bringing up of their children, their well-established reputation for hospitality, make them worthy of honor, and they may be enrolled as "real widows". But even here the solidity and realism of the writer's ethics are to be seen. Real widows of proven reputation and real need may be supported by the church. But if a widow has any relatives—children or grandchildren—theirs is the responsibility for her support. They are not to shirk that responsibility, for "if any one does not provide for his relatives, and especially for his own family, he has disowned the faith and is worse than an un-believer" (1 Timothy 5: 8). So important in his eyes is this injunction that in the next paragraph he repeats it: "If any believing woman has relatives who are widows, let her assist them; let the church not be burdened" (1 Timothy 5: 16). To many this seemed a strange word, and many manuscripts read instead "If any believing man or woman . . ." Textually the addition is suspicious as too easy, although adopted by many commentators and translators (as Easton and Moffatt). Probably what our author is saying is that instead of gadding about and demanding support for themselves the younger widows are to remarry, re-assume their proper responsibility in running their households, and provide support for those older who cannot fend for themselves.

Mention has already been made of the author's insistence that women be women and do not attempt to ape the role of the man. She is to "learn in silence with all submissiveness"; she is not "to teach or have authority over men"; instead she is to keep silent (1 Timothy 2: 11ff.). Seemingly this view, dated as it may seem to many to-day, was that of Paul (although occassionally scholars have regarded 1 Corinthians 14: 34f. as a passage added later, based on these words in 1 Timothy), and it can be easily understood as a protest against innovations of the most dangerous sort. The fact that among the most vicious of the false teachers were figures like Simon the Samaritan, who openly paraded the notorious Helena, while the belittling of marriage by those who practiced severe discipline made natural the role of teacher for women who renounced wedlock (cf. Thecla), is quite sufficient to account for the thorough-going restriction by our author.

Propriety in Worship

In our letters we have clear intimation of the necessity for propriety in the conduct of public worship. Once again our author is not spelling out in detail the precise way a service was to be conducted—he makes no reference at all to the Lord's Supper or Eucharist; no reference to the time or form of baptism—but he does throw light, both by explicit word and by his choice of phrases throughout the epistles, "how one ought to behave in the household of God" (1 Timothy 3 : 15). In this connection his words are revealing: "First of all, then, I urge that supplications, prayers, intercessions, and thanksgivings be made for all men, for kings and all who are in high positions . . ." (1 Timothy 2: 1f.). That this has to do with public worship, not private devotions, is evident as he continues: "I desire then that in 'every place' [that is, at every meeting] the men should pray, lifting holy hands without anger or quarreling" (2 : 8). Women, on the contrary, are to keep silent and to show their piety and that they have the spirit of prayer by their modest garb—no fancy hair-do, no gold ornaments, pearls, or costly garments—and seemly demeanor.

There is no indication of any special church buildings. Presumably Christians met for their services in the house of some member. Very probably the situation evident in Paul's letters (cf. 1 Corinthians 14) still prevailed, with all the men present permitted their share in the service. But there is no hint of the earlier confusion which often resulted and which led Paul to seek, without "quenching the Spirit", to safeguard some semblance of order. Presumably the actual form of the service followed the basic pattern inherited from the synagogue. Together with a minimizing of the ecstatic, being "carried away" by the Spirit, so common in the earlier days, is the clear evidence of at least a start towards a settled and conventional liturgy. Not improbably the words "for kings and all who are in high positions, that we may lead a quiet and peaceable life, godly and respectful in every way" (1 Timothy 2: 2), are to be seen as a definite bit of an actual prayer in use in public worship.

Frequently in these little epistles are phrases—some short, some long—which give the appearance of being quotations. Several of these are definitely quoted with the words: "The saying is sure" (1 Timothy 1: 15; 3: 1; 4: 9; 2 Timothy 2: 11; Titus 3: 8). Most of them would seem to be of what can be styled a liturgical sort.

> For there is one God,
> And there is one mediator between God and men,
> > The man Christ Jesus,
> > Who gave himself as a ransom for all,
> The testimony to which was borne at the proper time
> > > (1 Timothy 2: 5-6)

is certainly so to be regarded. Its five abrupt clauses are in marked contrast to the literary style of the rest of the letter and would seem a Christian equivalent of the Jewish *Shema* (Deuteronomy 6: 4f.). Certainly

> > He was manifested in the flesh,
> > Vindicated in the Spirit,
> > > Seen by angels,
> > Preached among the nations,
> > Believed on in the world,
> > > Taken up in glory   (1 Timothy 3: 16),

with its marked assonance, appears to be two three-line couplets from a hymn. There are at least three apparent citations from

77

what may be styled baptismal hymns (2 Timothy 1: 9–10; 2: 11b–13a; Titus 3: 5b–7), all of which might well be printed in a format to indicate their nature:

> Who saved us and called us
> > With a holy calling,
> Not in virtue of our works
> > But in virtue of his own purpose and the grace
> Which he gave us in Christ Jesus
> > Ages ago,
> And now has manifested
> > Through the appearing of our Savior
> Christ Jesus,
> > Who abolished death
> And brought life and immortality to light
> > Through the gospel   (2 Timothy 1: 9–10).

"If anyone aspires to the office of bishop, he desires a noble task" (1 Timothy 3: 1) may well be a phrase from the service of ordination. "Our blessed hope, the appearing of the glory of our great God and Savior Jesus Christ" (Titus 2: 13) is surely a fragment from a hymn or credal chant, as is the ornate doxology, "To the King of ages, immortal, invisible, the only God, be honor and glory for ever and ever. Amen" (1 Timothy 1: 17), which later is still further enriched at the conclusion of this same epistle (6: 15b–16).

Preservation of Values

These fragments (and the few which I have cited are not exhaustive), indicate what may be styled a growing concern for an orderly and sedate form of worship in which there is little place for the earlier ecstatic outbursts of emotional unrestraint, tolerated, but nonetheless feared, by Paul. No longer does the Church expect the end to come to-morrow. That the Lord will return was, of course, an orthodox inheritance; but no longer was it the driving force that it had been in the previous century. Christians might continue to be styled those who "love his appearing" (2 Timothy 4: 8), but during the lapse of the years they had settled down to wait for it.

Carefully selected leaders, exemplifying in their own lives the sort of conduct worthy of those whom God had led to a knowledge of the truth, a growing concern that the inherited values should not be lost or perverted, which made indispensable the careful instruction and testing of those who made the good confession—these were the new imperatives. "Whosoever will may come" might still be the Savior's gracious promise; but it entailed a careful oversight and evidence that they were in a position to "follow the pattern of the sound words" (2 Timothy 1: 13), which was the priceless heritage of the Church from the one who had so conspicuously "fought the good fight . . . finished the race . . . kept the faith" (2 Timothy 4: 7). The "deposit" which had been entrusted to the Timothys and Tituses and which must be kept without blemish or alteration was under attack by those who had appeared, as Paul had long ago prophesied that they would, and were seeking to pervert good morals by undermining the one sure foundation upon which sound religion rested.

The author may well be styled a conservative: his great fear is deviation from the one sure gospel which he and his fellows have received. There is, as has been constantly said, little of the pioneer in him. He is more than content to walk in the well-established paths; he is insistent that this be done, since any other course must end in disaster as it had in the past in the case of Hymenaeus and Alexander (1 Timothy 1: 20). But though little of the reformer is to be seen in him, he is no quiet or passive conservative, preferring to sit back and drink his old wine. Rather he is a very active and militant crusader. It is not that he wishes to better the old or to break new and more direct paths. That would be to him unthinkable. His crusade is against those whom he views with contempt, but nonetheless with alarm, who by their false doctrines and arrogant pretense to knowledge are making inroads and are causing so many to "turn away from listening to the truth and wander into myths" (2 Timothy 4:4). The Church stands for true religion. It must gird itself to the attack of all—and they are many—who are seeking to pervert that which has been committed to its charge.

5

"WAGE THE GOOD WARFARE"

THROUGHOUT THESE letters is a constant and direct attack upon false teachers. They are "empty talkers and deceivers" who for base gain are "teaching what they have no right to teach" (Titus 1: 10f.). They are "making their way into households and capturing weak women, burdened with sins" (2 Timothy 3: 6). They are puffed up with conceit, know nothing, have a morbid craving for controversy and for disputes about words (1 Timothy 6: 4). Their mouths must be stopped.

Only by determined opposition to such can the tradition be held inviolate and order be preserved in the churches. They must be sharply and decisively opposed; those whom they are leading astray must be effectively, if gently, corrected and made to cease from their desire to "accumulate for themselves teachers to suit their own likings" (2 Timothy 4: 3), must be made to see the folly of such a course.

Defend the Deposit

There can be but little question that it was the presence of such dangerous figures which led our author to compose, in the name of the long-dead Paul, his impassioned plea to guard the deposit. The danger, long before prophesied, has come. False teachers are making havoc in the fold. That they are to be seen as gnostics, not impossibly as followers of Marcion—properly himself not a gnostic, but easily included in their ranks—has been suggested on an earlier page (pp. 41–43). The way in which our second-century Paulinist attacks them and the particular teachings he deplores deserve a further word.

The contemptuous reference to their concern about "myths and endless genealogies" (1 Timothy 1 : 4; cf. Titus 3 : 9) was not misunderstood by Irenaeus, who, perhaps a generation later, used this phrase in the opening sentence of his devastating attack upon those men who have "set the truth aside and bring in lying words and vain genealogies, which . . . draw away the minds of the inexperienced and take them captive". Thus attempts to see the false teachers, against whom our author is set, as orthodox if hostile Jews are quite unwarranted. It is not the tiresome and wordy legends about the Jewish patriarchs—their pedigree and the profound depths of moral insight which a thinker like Philo could find, in the form of allegory, in his re-writing of the Old Testament. These might be profitless and absurd; they were neither vicious nor immoral, and could in no wise be regarded as imperiling the faith of immature Christians or leading them into moral evil. Our author's constant warning against the moral shipwreck certain, if these pretentious and vicious pilots be followed, is enough to make certain that it is not the teaching of the synagogue or the discoveries of learned would-be sitters in the seat of Moses that he is deploring.

To be sure, in his protest against "many empty talkers and deceivers" he adds "especially the circumcision party" (Titus 1 : 10), and a few verses later he adds a warning against "Jewish myths". It is not Judaism, but Gnosticism, which not infrequently adopted and perverted Biblical truth, against which he is crying out. Actually there could be no such thing as "Jewish Gnosticism". Aside from the fact that Gnosticism was basically dualistic (teaching that there were two supreme Powers) while Judaism was beyond question monistic (believing in one Power), Jewish ceremonial practices were such that were a Jew to adopt gnostic views he ceased to be a Jew. Occasionally this happened.

Simon Magus and his pupil, Menander, are often cited. But they were not Jews, nor was their teaching Jewish.

Gnosticism, as depicted in the pages of Irenaeus and now in our own time being seen in the horde of gnostic writings recently discovered in Egypt, does meet the situation so evident in our letters. The host of "emanations" (aeons)—thirty of them, with at least thirty-seven different names—which bridged the gulf between the world of matter and the altogether-other God devised by Valentinus, and tirelessly reported in all its endless detail (for the purpose of holding the absurd speculations up to ridicule) by Irenaeus, is the menace our author faces. These teachers, in their contempt for matter and confident of their "perfect knowledge", too frequently insisted, "To us, who are clean, everything is permitted, for nothing can defile us." And not infrequently, as Irenaeus makes but too clear, they put this theory into definite practice at the cost of many of their female converts.

Moreover, many of these gnostics could easily seem "would-be teachers of the law" in consequence of their perverse use of the Scriptures as indications, if not proofs, of their doctrines. Their tetrad (group of four divine beings) was indicated by the long robe of the priest, which was adorned by four rows of precious stones; their ogdoad (group of eight) by the eight persons saved in Noah's ark and the fact that David occupied eighth place in terms of age among his brothers; their decad (group of ten) by the fact that at the well Rebecca received ten bracelets of gold and that Jeroboam gained ten tribes. Similarly, as Irenaeus so bitterly complains: ". . . from the writings of the evangelists and the apostles they endeavour to derive proofs for their opinions by means of perverse interpretations and deceitful exposition."

To our author, all this is abhorrent, and from it he recoils. He is not a careful historian, seeking to analyse and understand divergent views. Instead, he is a very practical and down-to-earth guardian of what he is sure is ancient and God-given tradition endangered by godless and vicious men. Thus his sweeping injunction: "But avoid stupid controversies, genealogies, dissensions, and quarrels over the law, for they are unprofitable and futile" (Titus 3: 9). Paul would have shown in each case *why* they were vicious and futile, but our author was not Paul. Nor is it to be forgotten that quite probably his contemptuous reference, "especially the circumcision party", and his styling the delirium from which he recoils "Jewish myths", simply indicate a loose use of language, true in every age, for a hated opponent.

Another of the teachings of those errorists was their prohibition of foods and marriage: "who forbid marriage and enjoin abstinence from foods which God created to be received with thanksgiving" (1 Timothy 4: 3). That this is a protest against ascetic practices, not primarily an attack against Jewish dietary laws, is clear. In gnostic thought there is a determined and logically natural opposition both to marriage and to the use of meat and wine. The material world was evil, not the creation of God but the product of a being who in his blindness thought himself to be God, although in reality he was God's chief opponent. Thus marriage, which meant the production of new bodies, and the more material form of food—meat and wine—were to be avoided. To our author this was but another evidence of these teachings' Satanic origin. In short, it was a blasphemous repudiation of God, for it was God who had created all foods and who had enjoined marriage. Thus the clear-cut rule was sure: "Everything created by God is good, and nothing is to be re-

jected if it is received with thanksgiving" (1 Timothy 4: 4).
This was but in line with the obvious teaching of Scripture, with
its insistent refrain in the story of creation, "And God saw that
it was good."

Moreover, it had the clearest support in Paul. Had he not in
contempt repudiated the perverse teachings of those who were
upsetting the Colossians with their specious regulations: "Do
not handle, Do not taste, Do not touch"? (Colossians 2: 20–
23.) Moreover, in his word to the Corinthians, even more
clearly in the letter to Rome, had he not insisted that meat could
not of itself defile or injure the eater? It was not the meat which
could harm even a "weak" Christian, but the doing of something, itself innocent, contrary to the fears of conscience by those
whose knowledge was imperfect. Apparently this nice point
escapes our author; or rather, his modification "by those who
believe and know the truth" suggests that for him this more
"sensible" knowledge is the possession of all mature Christians.
No longer is the situation which confronted Paul—the "weak"
and the "strong"—to be found. The two sides are now of a
sort where no compromise is possible. Had not Paul long ago
protested against these perverse and man-made restrictions?
Thus he is certain that, were Paul alive and confronting this new
attempt to jettison the Church of the living God, he would but
have repeated his protest. And this outlook, both scriptural and
thoroughly Pauline, was highly congenial to our author, who so
manifestly was completely at home in a world where the golden
mean was the ideal and who disliked excess in every form.

Beware of Strange Teachings

It is highly probable that in our author's eyes the Jewish
dietary restrictions are also lifted, for by his day the distinction in
Christian eyes between "clean" and "unclean" had long since

lapsed. Some commentators have wondered that our author does not cite the gospel word, "Whatever goes into a man from outside cannot defile him," and the appended conclusion, "Thus he declared all foods clean" (Mark 7: 18f.), as Paul appears to have done (Romans 14: 14). Apparently he is content to rest his contention upon God's purpose in creation. Nonetheless his feeling is not against what is and what is not "kosher"—that is now far in the past—rather his attack is upon a very lively peril, the teachings of those who "abstain from animal food and draw away multitudes by a feigned temperance of this kind" (Irenaeus, *Against Heresies* i, 24, 2).

The matter is even clearer in regard to marriage. Here there can be no question of opposition to Jewish error. For the Synagogue the injunction of God stood sacrosanct: "Be fruitful and multiply." But this was not the teaching of Gnosticism or of Marcion. For them marriage was to be avoided. For some gnostics, as has been suggested, this instruction by no means prevented the most flagrant sexual wrong-doings, for all this was but another way of showing contempt for the vile material body. For Marcion, unlike many other gnostics with whom he has been uncritically classed, not only was marriage to be avoided, but all sexual activity was frowned upon. It was precisely because of his exemplary moral standards that Marcion was regarded as so dangerous, for, as Origen was to remark, the most dangerous heretics are those whose lives are good.

Thus the heated attack upon those who forbid marriage, together with the unmodified approbation of—if actually not insistence upon—marriage for Christians, both clerical and lay, would seem entirely consistent and natural if, as is far from improbable, our author finds himself opposed to the teaching of the one who so confidently but unwarrantedly claimed to be the one man who both understood and followed in the steps of Paul.

It is also possible that our author's flat denial of the right of

86

women to teach—instead, their function was severely restricted, as was to be the case under another régime, to church-children-kitchen—while in agreement with the traditional word of Paul, was heightened by the already dawning suspicion of the superiority of virginity to marriage and in inevitable consequence of the dangerous preference of some Christian Theclas for a renunciation of marriage and adoption of a life devoted to preaching the word.

The Place of the Resurrection

One other teaching of these dangerous destroyers of the flock of God may be mentioned, namely, that attributed to Hymenaeus and Philetus, that the "resurrection is past already" (2 Timothy 2: 18). To Greeks, as is so strikingly brought out in Paul's speech in Athens before the Areopagus, the notion of a resurrection of dead bodies was alien. When the idea of life after death came to be accepted, it was in terms of the very different immortality of the soul. This view was the natural consequence of the growing belief that the body (*sōma*) was the tomb (*sēma*) of the soul, and in direct contrast to the belief in later Judaism that future life must of necessity involve the restoration of the body.

It was precisely at this point that Paul had had such difficulties. With his Jewish heritage he found it impossible to envisage future life apart from a body; his experience as a missionary to Greeks confronted him with the task of translating this view into intelligible and acceptable terms. It was in consequence of this that he seems to have reached his compromise view of a "spiritual body", which has so perplexed his many disciples through the ages.

To gnostics, with their conviction that matter was in itself evil, all thought of resurrection was abhorrent. The real significance of salvation was that it freed one for all time and in all degree from the alien body. Both Irenaeus and Justin assert that Menander, the successor of Simon Magus, taught that his disciples obtained resurrection through "being baptized into him" and in consequence would never die. In the present passage (2 Timothy 2: 18) the view attributed to Hymenaeus and Philetus seems to be a bit different: the resurrection has already occurred. The precise origin of this view is uncertain. Should it be styled "gnostic" or "Christian gnostic"? Is it that the soul has now been reborn from some earlier life or is it that since it is by faith in Christ that men gain immortal life the resurrection will not be delayed until after death but has already taken place? In this connection the emphasis in the Gospel of John cannot be disregarded, with its insistence: "I am the Resurrection and the Life" (11: 25). To what extent the author of those words has been influenced by gnostic thought is far from clear, but the possibility is real that in gnostic circles the idea was expressed in less veiled and guarded terms.

The possibility is not to be overlooked that the matter is further complicated. One of the main objects of the Fourth Gospel is to support Christian faith at a point where it was being sorely tried. The expected bodily return of Jesus, long the mainspring of the Christian movement, had not been realized. The contribution of "John" was a brave but desperate one: "We have been wrong in so understanding Jesus' promise. It has been realized. He came, as He had promised; He came when after His resurrection He met His disciples and breathed on them His spirit." This view, in many eyes to-day the veriest orthodoxy, was heresy writ large when it was first expressed, and the gospel encountered grave opposition.

To me it has long seemed probable that it is only in this connection that 2 Thessalonians can be understood. No serious reader of that letter can fail to be pulled up short by the amazing statement—in the eyes of all interpreters the pivotal point in the letter—"We beg you, brethren, not to be quickly shaken in mind or excited, either by spirit or by word, or by letter purporting to be from us, to the effect *that the day of the Lord has come*" (2 Thessalonians 2: 2). That Paul's earlier letter to them, not to mention his oral preaching, could have led to such an understanding is not easy to accept. Had, however, the Fourth Gospel appeared with its insistence that the day of the Lord had indeed come—that is, that there would never be His expected celestial advent on the clouds—it is far from impossible that a zealous Paulinist should have sought to have refuted such horrid heresy.

To me the possibility is real that our author, knowing 2 Thessalonians, which he accepted without question as from the pen of Paul, found it a support for the problem at the moment confronting him, viz., men once again mistakenly asserting that the resurrection is past, that is, in Pauline terms, that the Lord had already returned.

"Knowledge Versus Faith"

Nor should his word, following his reference to this outrageous view, be overlooked: Folks who so teach "are upsetting" the faith of some. In his day, as has already been remarked, the expected Second Coming (parousia) was by no means the all-important spur to Christian thinking and living that it had earlier been. Nevertheless it remained, as it has in subsequent generations, a promise to be realized in God's good time. Its denial was outrageous. Did it not tacitly deny the all-important and steadying belief in a future final judgment? Would not such a denial irremediably endanger Christian morals, already in some circles weakened? Against such a menace he cried aloud in protest, and in his word he may well have thought that he was but repeating Paul's own word of horror at those who would jettison all Christian faith by saying that "there is no resurrection of the dead" (1 Corinthians 15: 12).

As he saw these wolves, some in sheep's clothing, endangering the flock, destroying the faith, he took up the pen of his master to insist to the men of his day, as he knew Paul would have done: "Guard what has been entrusted to you. Avoid the godless chatter and contradictions of what is falsely called knowledge, for by professing it some have missed the mark as regards the faith" (1 Timothy 6: 20f.).

6

ABIDING VALUES OF THE LETTERS

WE ARE very fortunate that these little writings to Timothy and Titus are a part of our sacred Scriptures. To many modern readers this unmodified statement may seem surprising, if not actually wrongheaded. The constant insistence on "guarding the tradition", the endless harping on "sound doctrine", the contemptuous dismissal of anything approaching speculative thinking as "godless chatter", "disputes about words", "stupid and senseless controversies" which are "unprofitable and futile" —all this seems to strike an alien note.

Never once throughout his writing does the author seem to find any problem crying to be solved; never does he appear to have the slightest inclination towards anything that even suggests curiosity. Instead, he seems to know all he wants to know. There are no secrets beyond the horizon to be searched for, not even a Pisgah to be climbed for a glimpse into the Promised Land beyond Jordan. He is not a prophet; God has not whispered or shouted in his ear a new and demanding message. Worse than that, this lack does not seem to bother him in the slightest. He is not intellectually adventurous and is stubbornly hostile to all who are. What values, then, can be found in such an outlook?

A Picture of our Early Brethren

The writings are of very great value to those who are interested in the past, in particular the early days of our religion. It is true that while he is steeped in Pauline thought he constantly fails to understand Paul's thinking. Though ever seeking to under-stand Paul—and seemingly quite sure that he is entirely successful—again and again it is evident that he has fallen far short of his ideal. Nonetheless he reveals the very great influence that Paul has had upon him, and that in the thought of those to whom he writes Paul stands as no hazy figure of the long-ago past but as one who though dead still is speaking. One cannot read these epistles and still toy with the notion that Paul's importance was but a later, if not actually recent, discovery.

These little writings lift the roofs of many churches in the second century and let us see our early brethren as they were, unconscious that they are being watched. No longer are they expecting at any moment to hear the heavenly trumpet—tomorrow, next week, next month. Rather, Christians are finding themselves in a world which seems of a nature to endure, and this situation has brought many new demands.

In this situation one thing is clear to our author. The ultimate concern of the churches is and must be a religious one. There must be right organization, high moral standards, but these all depend on a genuine and abiding faith in God. As the church stands for religion, it must of necessity stand for the true religion, must hold this true against all attempts at perversion, and they are many, which are seeking to undermine and destroy what God has for all time revealed. This had been communicated by none other than God to Paul as his most precious trust and responsibility. It is to be kept unsullied, and to be transmitted by a series of consecrated and devoted leaders.

The lesson too often overlooked to-day in our eagerness to pass value judgments is that before we reach our verdict "good" or "bad", knowledge of what we would appraise is absolutely necessary. Here these letters are invaluable. They may tell us little of the first-century Paul, may preserve little or nothing of otherwise unknown historical traditions of his life, but they reveal, as few other writings we have do, the life and thought—problems and attempted answers—of our early brethren in what may be styled not alone the "second century" of Christianity, but also the "second breath". The first age was past—that of the pioneers and road breakers. Mounting with wings was over; it was a time of walking without growing weary.

Discipline of the Christian Army

More than that, it was a time when men like our author were sorely needed; in a word, a time for drill sergeants who could whip the new recruits into line and turn them into soldiers. Rules were necessary. Then as now, freedom without rules spells anarchy. And many of his rules were wholesome ones. The mystic may feel a sense of loss. Our author does not see visions and only infrequently dreams dreams.

His concern was with the common people—very plentiful, then as now—who were finding in their new loyalties a type of life incomparably higher and more demanding than that to which they had been accustomed, and who needed constant encouragement and warning.

The time was yet to come—although it came speedily—when Christianity was to become "intellectually respectable" through the efforts of men like Clement and, in a measure, Origen. Fortunate it is that this had been preceded by a time of solid foundation building. The genius of Christianity—and for it she is deeply indebted to the Synagogue which gave her birth—is her solid ethical foundation. Upon that a superstructure might eventually be reared. Without it the imposing house and roof would have tumbled to the ground.

Upon this foundation our author labored and successfully. Granted that his demands were moderate, that his ethics were of the middle-of-the-road and common-sense type. That was what was needed then, nor is the need conspicuously absent to-day.

Nor is it too profound criticism to wave him aside with such descriptions as "stodgy" and "pedestrian". Granted that he is content to act as a bellhop, passing on the luggage from the past to the present. It should not be forgotten, in such an easy quip, that not all that is "old" is worthless. Tradition may at times be described in terms of the throttling hold of the neck of the future by the dead hands of the past. That is not all that it is, by any means. Tradition can also be a lifeline, without which one can easily flounder and drown when the waves are high and the winds strong.

Christian Responsibility

Many of the emphases he passed on—the need for a wholesome purity of life, both in teacher and taught; the demand for a reputation (as well as character) above reproach; the unanswerable, and often quite forgotten, insistence that unless a man is able to bring up and train (he called it "rule") his own household, it is not likely that he will be a great success in "bringing up and training" a church; the demand that a man or woman feel responsibility, and put said responsibility into action, for the support of his own family—these, and they are but few of the wholesome touches, are just as relevant to-day as they were when he crossed his last Greek "t".

The fact that in keeping with his own day he sought to write in the person and style of his revered master Paul led of necessity to a certain artificiality. To no small extent it has hidden the man himself from us. To no small extent that is a pity, for he would have been a man well worth knowing. It is highly probable that he was a man far easier to live with than were many who far outranked him in intellectual adventuresomeness.

He was also a keen observer, not easily fooled, unconcerned

with tilting at windmills or shadow-boxing with straw men. Those with whom he was concerned were real people, and he was alike able shrewdly to appraise them and deftly to describe them. And many of them are to be found in our day as they were in his: the pompous and self-sure intoners of windy nothingness; silly women with nothing to do, gadding from one church—or cult— to another, sermon tasters always eager for a new thrill, but with no comprehension of what they were hearing; those who were quick to join for the practical advantages, both social and financial, of becoming members of an organization from which they might expect dividends; folk who carried right practices to such foolish extremes and excesses as to make vices of them and fools of themselves. All of these appear in his pages, and to each his words are apt.

To revert to my opening word: we are very fortunate that these little writings are a part of our sacred Scriptures. They may not seem the strong meat to be found in the earlier letters of Paul and in the gospels; but to continue that figure, salt is a very necessary preservative and has a place in a balanced diet. And these letters are salt, and of a sort that does not quickly lose its savor.

To change the figure—with an eye to Paul's oft-quoted words about different members of the body, each of value, each necessary to a properly functioning whole—in an orchestra there is a need for instruments not intended for solo parts. Without them the ensemble is sadly out of balance. So in the writings of the New Testament there is a place—and an honored place—for these quite unpretentious but abidingly wholesome writings which lay stress on values, often overlooked and for- gotten, but which still continue to be values without which we would be a deal the poorer.